Building
Brandwidth

Also by Sergio Zyman:

The End of Marketing As We Know It

BUILDING
Brandwidth

CLOSING
THE SALE
ONLINE

SERGIO ZYMAN
and Scott Miller

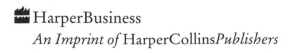

HarperBusiness
An Imprint of HarperCollins*Publishers*

To Denise from both of us

HarperCollins books may be purchased for educational, business, or sales promotional use. For information please write: Special Markets Department, HarperCollins Publishers Inc., 10 East 53rd Street, New York, NY 10022.

FIRST EDITION

Designed by Stratford Publishing Services

Printed on acid-free paper

Library of Congress Cataloging-in-Publication Data

Zyman, Sergio.
    Building brandwidth : closing the sale online / Sergio Zyman and
    Scott Miller.—1st ed.
        p. cm.
    Includes index.
    ISBN 0-06-662060-0 (alk. paper)
    1. Internet marketing   I. Miller, Scott, 1945–   II. Title.
    HF5415.1265 .Z95 2000
    658.8'4 21; aa05 07-14—dc00   00-058185

---

00 01 02 03 04   RRD   10 9 8 7 6 5 4 3 2 1

CONTENTS

INTRODUCTION

The point of my last book, *The End of Marketing As We Know It*, was inescapable. After all, it was meant to be a two-by-four to the side of the head for everybody in marketing. Yo! It's time to write the new rules of marketing. It's time to start demanding results, not just fluff. Marketing makes global commerce work. The incredible intensification of competition in every market and the ever increasing clutter of information in every consumer's mind have made the process of marketing more important than ever. **Marketing must make something happen: It's got to sell stuff.** In other words, marketing has to work harder than ever. And, if it's not working, kill it. Period.

It's the end of marketing as the toy box of corporate org charts. It's the end of marketing departments' excesses and excuses. It's the end of marketing departments that are little more than an advertising agency manager. Yeah, that means some of the good times are definitely over. You must treat marketing as serious business. That doesn't mean it's not fun—there's nothing funner than winning in the marketplace. Just hold the celebrations until AFTER the game, please, not while you're still trying to get the ball over the fifty yard line.

Today, marketing is just too important to be left only to marketing people—it is the job of virtually everyone in virtually any organization, because the job of marketing is to add value to any transaction. Who shouldn't be part of that? It's the job of product development, manufacture, operations, accounting, sales, distribution, HR (human resources), customer relationship management, merchandising, advertising, PR, investor relations—everyone. If you've opened this book, it's obviously your job, too, or you feel it should be. And you're interested in doing it better. **You want to get people to come back more often to buy more from you and be willing to pay more for it.**

That's a tough job anytime. And in this hypercompetitive environment, no marketing activity is neutral. If your marketing is not creating value, it's subtracting it, while the competition is moving up or even past you. You've got to be on the job 24-7.

This book is written by me and Scott Miller, my long-term friend. We wanted to tell you what's been happening since *The End of Marketing,* the new rules and instructions that we are applying and recommending to all of our clients: BAMs (bricks and mortars), dot.coms, and BAM.coms. Marketing is now being rethought and reevaluated. (Maybe *The End of Marketing* did serve as a wake-up call for some people!)

In this book we take the concepts from *The End of Marketing* far ahead, showing you the most effective way to close the sale online again and again—this is building brandwidth. Eventually, every company on the Internet is going to have to succeed in doing this. They're going to have to sell stuff, and sell more and more of it: This isn't dot.communism. **More and more often these days you hear about investors' flight to quality and away from skittish Internet shares. The quality they're flying to is called profits.** And profits come only when you sell more stuff to more people more often for more money. In other words, they only come when you master the art and science of marketing.

When you've mastered marketing, you've developed a brand: the thick, rich relationship between customers and your product, service, or company. You've developed the long-lasting dialogue that actually builds dimensionality into the meaning of a brand. In the new economy, this means you've changed your way of thinking of and doing business. You've built brandwidth. You're making money in the new economy.

At our strategy house, Z Group, it's our *jihad* to help our clients worldwide to get marketing done the way it should be done, to get the results it must get, to address the serious business issues it must address.

About two years ago, we began to be approached by a new kind of client: much younger, unestablished in the world of business, technologically astute, but sometimes undisciplined about the most basic business processes, energized and excited about the coming online revolution, highly caffeinated and wound to the tightness of the high C on a piano. They would ask us, "Now that we've funded our concept and launched it, something is wrong. Nobody showed up to see it. What's the problem?" We were also approached by the people who fund these young entrepreneurs. One thing these people certainly don't lack is aggressive competitiveness. You've heard me say it before: Everything communicates and everything markets. And on the Net, everything you do has consequence. So this has the psychological rewards of the political consulting work we've done—you do something right (or wrong) and it makes stuff happen . . . real fast!

Among the youngbloods who approached us were a few supersmart young businessmen from Philadelphia, Walter Buckley, Ken Fox, and Doug Alexander of ICG, or Internet Capital Group. Their vision extended even beyond the Net, to a revolution of the world of investment banking and venture capital. These men and their colleagues were the pioneers in developing the B2B (business-to-business) side of e-commerce, which has quickly overshadowed the consumer side in scope and penetration. Already, Internet-based B2B commerce is being conducted by almost 35% of all U.S. businesses and accounts for more than 10% of *all* business commerce. Forrester Research estimates that by 2003 the B2B e-commerce space will account for more than $3 trillion of our total economy—maybe $7 trillion by 2007.

IGC is at the forefront of this movement. Their focus isn't on either the "new economy" or the "old economy": It's firmly fixed on the transformed economy that will emerge as the Internet matures and goes through consolidation and integration—the great shake-out. It'll be traditional BAMs and Web startups working and competing together. ICG is actively involved throughout the life of its portfolio companies. ICG represents a new holistic vision of shareholder activism, taking strong positions in its portfolio companies and providing a corporate hub of state-of-the-Internet services and support (legal, HR, IT corporate strategy, marketing, PR) to make sure those portfolio companies grow and prosper. ICG has a strong operating focus and is actively engaged in B2B e-commerce through a network of partner companies. The men and women of ICG are supersmart (to use Bill Gates's compliment) and superfocused. It's no wonder that so far they've been supersuccessful, too.

We've worked with ICG and many of their portfolio companies during this remarkable sea change in American business. In addition to our work with ICG's partner companies—Commerx, Tradex, EmployeeLife, Deja, Computerjobs, BuyMedia, NetVendor, InvestorForce, Breakaway Solutions, and others—we've worked with Broadband Sports, LastMinuteTravel, e-Hatchery, VETxchange, Industry Networks, Nexchange, OmniPod, eTour, MGISoftware, Google, Netcentives, and others.

When this book goes to press, we'll be developing work with ten more companies. We've gone onto the Net ourselves with zmarketing.com, extending the reach of our thinking, marketing principles and Z Group's consulting work, while providing new Internet-enabled marketing tools and the first true marketing marketplace, bringing buyers and suppliers together from every aspect of this multibillion dollar industry.

We were at ground zero of this unique event, the development and deployment worldwide of the Internet, the culmination of the worldwide information revolution. This revolution is the force that is changing literally everything in our lives: business, politics, entertainment, education, science, warfare, and sex. It was the information revolution, not political policy, that brought down the Iron Curtain. As early as 1985, the height of power and menace of the "Evil Empire," Scott's former political client, the brilliant Pat Moynihan, observed, "The Soviet Union is over. The Soviet Union faces an impossible choice. The world economy is being increasingly driven by information. They can decide to let it in and face certain political chaos. Or they can decide to try to keep it out and fall back into the dark ages of the industrial revolution."

Through Mikhail Gorbachev's glasnost policies, the Soviet Union tried to do both at once: let information in and limit its effects. It had the same result as jamming down both the accelerator and brakes on a speeding car. The Soviet Union ended up in the ditch.

Gorbachev proved one of our principles of marketing in this information economy: Reinvent or die. Incremental change doesn't do the job.

The Internet represents the real promise of this revolution. And much of the chaos, too. The Internet may be the perfect marketing machine, but it's a machine that needs master mechanics. It provides access to opportunity and choice for buyers and sellers worldwide, instantly, 24-7. Often there's not time to get it perfect, because you've just plain got to get it done. You often have to commit to ideas that are still greasy, screaming babes out of the womb. It may represent a real step forward for the practice of marketing, but that step must be onto the solid foundation of business basics. Already a number of Internet companies have plunged through the thin ice into the frigid waters of marketplace reality.

If the Internet doesn't start selling more stuff more often to more people—in other words, if it doesn't start taking marketing seriously and practicing it seriously—a lot of nifty little Internet start-ups are going to be nifty little Internet bellyups. e-Marketing isn't just about building awareness, or likeability, or purchase intent. It's about moving the consumer to the sale.

The same principles apply as readily to bricks and mortar marketing as chips and clicks marketing. The world of marketing, the whole universe of marketing, is changing, simply because the Internet and the hype in and around it are changing what all consumers expect from all marketers in every category.

The Internet can be a little off-putting, we realize. The ups and downs and inversions have the stomach-wrenching effect of the Batman loop-de-loop at Six Flags. But it's all really just a battle for brandwidth. That's what the landgrab stakes of this battle are all about. Investors are willing to place their bets right now on the brands that are going to lead and dominate the markets of tomorrow. Which brand is going to elbow its way to the front of the pack in your category? Will it be a traditional brand leader or an Internet-enabled startup upstart? Which brand is going to have the stamina to stay there through the competitive free-for-all, the consolidations and fragmentations that will happen one after another? Will your brand be at the top of the heap? Will your brand keep explaining and reexplaining why people should buy your stuff and want to keep coming back more often to buy more of it? Will your brand be ready to climb over the growing pile of "me, too!"s in your marketplace?

Everybody in and around the Internet—managers, techies, journalists, investors or analysts—knows that there will be only two or three, at the most, winners in any category. Investors are betting right now on that outcome, maybe a five- or ten-year process . . . or maybe only a year or two in your category. It's a battle royal, and the chief weapon will be marketing and branding. The more brand-width you build, the more ammo you take into the battle.

Technology is very important, of course. Management principles play a key role. Product development is essential. But, let's face it, you and I know that it's marketing that's going to be the real difference between winning and losing.

Scott and I want you to be one of the winners (you bought, begged, borrowed, or stole our book, after all). We want you to be able to fight hard and fight smart, so we're giving you the best and latest equipment. Consider this book your user's manual of e-marketing.

We show you the initial forays into marketing by the new economy pioneers and help you understand the new forces in marketing and how they're being used by some of the most successful companies on the Net. We give you the fundamental principles of e-marketing and the most important result of e-marketing: building brandwidth. In the polluted space of e-commerce, brand is king, queen, prince, princess, and emperor. Building brandwidth is the way out of the nowhere land of sameness and confusion of competitive brands and competitive claims. It's about defining brands, connecting people to them, and enhancing their value on the Internet and everywhere else. This is your job, whatever your job title on the Internet.

We will help you understand and learn how to apply those e-marketing basics in this "new new thing," as author Michael Lewis has called it. If you're interested in getting sales, not advertising awards, you came to the right book. If you want to close the sale online or offline, if you want results RIGHT THIS SECOND, you came with the right attitude. Fasten your seat belt and read on!

Sergio Zyman

1

NOW WHAT?

We're sitting in this abandoned Pizza Hut in the middle of a fairly seedy shopping center south of San Francisco, trying to get our bearings. The walls are cheap sheetrock, just recently nailed up and now filled with unintelligible graffiti. Coffee-stained gray cubicle walls salvaged from a failed savings and loan divide the small space into a rabbit warren. The glow of a couple dozen PC screens plays over the cubicle field like the Aurora borealis. The CEO is sitting there in running shorts. The CFO, Starbucks Rich Colombian coursing through his veins, is emitting an audible buzz . . . he hasn't slept in thirty-some hours. Talking to them, we feel like faculty advisors in a student council meeting.

That was the beginning. The CEO in the shorts was worth something like $200 million at the time. A couple years later, at the end of April 2000, he was worth about a hundredth of that. Not that he really cared. This is revolution, not "Who Wants To Be A Millionaire?"

They were typical of the little startups we'd meet in those days, the first phase of Internet development. In those meetings, we'd be introduced to four or five software developers and engineers—one of them would be the designated "marketing guy."

"Well, Spencer, here, is our marketing department," the CEO says, indicating a guy with a buzz cut and goatee. "He's a code developer, but he used to be on a product marketing team at Sun. And he hired our ad agency. And they did the ad with the monkeys. Maybe you saw it."

We saw it, all right. We saw that they burned all of their first year's revenues on an ad campaign that never moved the needle. That explains what we were doing there in that strange place and a lot of other strange places. We were sitting there in that born-again Pizza Hut doing e-marketing.

THE NASDAQ ROCKET THUMBS ITS NOSE

Yes, some Internet companies achieved breathtaking valuations without selling anything. Back in the fall and winter of 1999 and 2000, EVERYBODY was rich, it seemed. Thirty-year-old Internet geniuses were picking out the carpeting for their Gulfstream Vs. And we all got a chance to see what our net worth would look like on steroids. It was an impressive sight: BIG . . . ENORMOUS . . . HUMONGOUS!

Valuations were still up there in the stratosphere. And it seemed you could IPO a can of tuna with a business model that could be written in very big letters on a very small bumper sticker. But somewhere in the pit of your stomach and seeping into the back of your mind was the poisonous thought: This can't really be; it wasn't really meant to be this easy. And a distant voice was warning that building valuation is a lot different from building real value. It's the difference between sand castles and brick outhouses. But at the time that voice seemed so distant, and it was drowned out by so many other voices, closer and so much more pleasant and so confident that the skyrocketing NASDAQ would just continue to rise against gravity, thumbing its rocket red nose at the laws of nature and finance and history.

Marketing advice was often pretty hard to sell in those heady days. "Do market research? Pound out a brand positioning strategy? What a downer! Let's just do some commercials!"

The marketing people of the time weren't focused on closing the sale online. They didn't even think about building brandwidth. Heck, they didn't have to sell stuff to get rich—all they had to do was IPO!

So hefty ad budgets bankrolled television commercials and full-page ads in the *New York Times* aimed at a market of a few hundred market analysts, not a few million consumers.

It seemed like everybody in and around the Internet was taking Tarzan pills, beating their chests and feeling invincible. And it was the end of business etiquette and business discipline as we'd known it. You couldn't get a phone call returned. Even e-mail wasn't returned. Due diligence? That's for nut companies buying bolt companies, not Net companies flying high in the ether. "We're different. We don't live by P&Ls, for gosh sakes. We've got funding." And discipline? Discipline is for dopes—marketing strategy is okay, but it takes too long. Hire an agency, do an ad for the Super Bowl. How hard is THAT?!

Our marketing advice for discipline, strategy, and process (after all, that's our business) seemed like a very long, uphill run for a lot of these people. Way too hard. No thanks.

FREEFALL BITES

The reality of a 40% NASDAQ freefall hit us all on April 24, 2000. The law of marketing gravity always applies eventually: If you can't sell stuff, you crash to earth. A lot of Internet companies did just that in the spring and summer of 2000, and now, like it or not, the little companies among them had to answer those nagging questions we'd kept asking them: "What is it you actually DO? And how are you going to make MONEY?"

They couldn't avoid it any longer.

The carnage was everywhere. And the higher flying the ego, it seemed, the farther and scarier the freefall. As the *Wall Street Journal* commented aptly, "Reality bites hard."

Sites had traffic, but no revenues. Iaminvincible.com suddenly became Ijustranoutofcash.com. After all, the convention of pricing in B2C (business to commerce) on the Internet was . . . FREE! Free services and free information. COME AND GET IT! In several of the "Little Rascals" films of the 1930s and 1940s, Spanky and Alfalfa decided to put on a show with Alfalfa crooning and Darla playing the ukulele, but the kids in the neighborhood balked at the penny admission price. Alfalfa invariably came up with the same plan: "I've got it! It'll be 'Pay As You Leave.'"

Well, the little rascals on the Web tried the same thing with the same results. Making people pay would discourage traffic. And traffic is what the funding angels and venture capitalists were looking at in those days. It would be like retailers at the mall getting credit for window shoppers. Ridiculous. But those were pretty ridiculous days.

Every B2C business plan we saw seemed to be predicting 25% of its revenues from advertising. Those same companies were devising television ad campaigns to build traffic, since Web advertising didn't do the job. Makes a lot of sense, right? At the time, it did.

Reality bit, and it was followed by another "ity" word: finality. By May, some of the splashiest B2C sites had gone bellyup, like Boo.com and Violet.com. All GONE! Sites like drkoop.com and CDnow.com were predicted to soon follow. (They got bought out for a fraction of the investment and initial IPO price.) All over the

Internet, the warning signs were flashing, like that worrisome little yellow gas pump on the dashboard of your car: "We're running out!" How can THAT be?

Well, there was the little problem of having no consumer proposition, no reason to buy, no relevance, no differentiation, and, hence, no sales or profit or customers.

There were some sober board meetings. It was like going to the principal's office, but worse. People began to use the "p" word again. "But we've still got great traffic. The only problem is profits."

Right. One little problem: No revenues. The "t" word was out.

In early April, we received an e-mail from Adrian Zackheim, the head of HarperBusiness at HarperCollins, our editor and good friend. "Any chance you could put the word 'profitability' in the book's subtitle?" Adrian wanted to know.

It was a sign of the times.

MARKETING—THE PICKS AND SHOVELS OF THE GOLD RUSH

A lot of Internet prospectors woke up with a megawatt hangover. Suddenly they realized that it was going to take backbreaking work just to get by, let alone succeed. They were going to have to dig hard and deep for the "P" in "P&L." And a lot of people realized that marketing would be the picks and shovels they'd have to use.

To be fair, nobody had exactly been hectoring these startups about the need to make money. Proformas tended to range between a best guess and a fervent wish. Virtually overnight, boards of directors that had previously acted like cheerleaders were now acting like referees: "Show us some proof that these numbers are HARD projections. When are you going to be making money?"

"Making money? Someday."

"WHICH someday?!"

Right about that moment, the designated marketing guy sure wished he could have back that $2 million he spent on the Super Bowl.

For a long time, most Internet company marketing, whether B2C or B2B (business-to-business), consisted of building name awareness. "The best-known name wins."

But who DOESN'T know DrKoop.com? Who doesn't remember Boo.com or Toysmart.com? There's nothing like a front-page obituary in the *Wall Street Journal* to get you awareness.

Name awareness is a pretty poor measure of brand strength. That's obvious, isn't it? Were they building purchase intent? Were they increasing brand loyalty the old-fashioned way, by increasing usage and repeat purchase? Were they maximizing customer value?

No. They were doing Super Bowl ads, building awareness. The *Wall Street Journal* reported that 38% of e-tailers had actually broken into the black, a pretty amazing figure. But the cost of acquisition per customer was sky-high: more than $80 a head, relative to $11 per customer for traditional catalogue companies moving online.

Wall Street quickly fell out of love with the entire B2C category. "Too risky," pronounced the same people who'd helped build those towering valuations in the first place. Those window-shoppers didn't account for any revenue. And those early category killers were suddenly standing among huge crowds of brands that looked, talked, acted, and smelled just like them. The ad revenue on their sites turned out to be "just a little optimistic." KABOOM!

Suddenly, B2B companies were the darlings of the analysts: no consumer acquisition costs, no false hopes of ad revenues. All you needed to do was disintermediate, and then reintermediate an existing process (you didn't have to invent a NEW one . . . just Webify an existing one).

Just as suddenly the B2Bs fell out of favor, because of the advent of the BAM (bricks-and-mortar) consortia. Analysts now said these old-line companies would transform their businesses using technology. And then it was the infrastructure companies' turn to come into favor, Ariba, Commerce One, i2, Oracle, and Breakaway Solutions.

It was like trying to keep track of a fifteen-year-old girl's boyfriends.

Then the NASDAQ hit the floor, and it didn't discriminate: It took everyone—B2C and B2B and B2CB and the BAM consortia and the infrastructure companies—with it into the sub-basement. A lot of highflyers awakened on this cold, hard stone floor, aware all of a sudden that they were just small businesses struggling against the traditional 80% failure rate of ALL small businesses. Bruised and battered, the Web executives realized that the only way out of there was to build a staircase of solid rock. Enter marketing. Enter positioning. Enter business plans grounded on facts, not hopes.

Suddenly at Z Group not only were we getting calls returned, but the phone was ringing off the hook. "You've got mail" brought another twenty inquiries daily.

The marketing meetings that resulted from those inquiries were very different from the meetings of just a few months before. Yes, the CEO was still in running shorts. And Starbucks Rich Colombian was still coursing through the CFO's veins. But now when we met to talk about marketing discipline, strategy, and process, people weren't wincing; they were listening attentively. "Show us where you keep the picks and shovels."

And it wasn't just Internet startups. Our experience is built on many years of corporate and political marketing consulting, and our relationships have been with the bluest of the blue chips: Coke, McDonald's, Microsoft, and News Corp. Now the BAMs moving to the Internet were calling, too. They were establishing e-procurement systems and e-supply chains. Some of them, like General Motors with Commerce One, were building huge e-marketplaces to include everyone in their value chain, from consumers to dealers to suppliers. Virtually every big BAM was at least looking at the Internet, and Forrester Research reported that in more than 40% of BAMs with a B2B task force, the task force was led by the CEO. You can bet the CEO felt the board of directors breathing down his or her neck: the stakes are high.

That said, the BAMs were moving to the Net with more than a little trepidation. Before the NASDAQ fall, you were considered a wuss if you weren't planning on building a marketplace and spinning it off into that updraft of NASDAQ valuations, but now BAM execs were seeing Internet companies falling from the sky around them. WAAAAAAAAAAAA! It was pretty daunting for the button-down managers. They were moving to the Internet all right, but kicking and screaming all the way.

And a funny thing happened to a lot of the BAMs' e-supply chains and marketplaces . . . nothing! Where was the activity? Whither the liquidity they'd been promised? Where the demand?

Many of them, it seemed, had forgotten one little detail when they assembled the e-marketplace . . . marketing. Without it, when they plugged in their new e-supply chain infrastructure and stepped back, it just sat there blinking at them.

It was like personal computers in the 1980s. The manufacturers got thousands of calls a day from people complaining, "I plugged in my new computer and nothing happens. It just sits there blinking at me." Whereupon the support people, with varying degrees of condescension, would inform the new owners that they'd have to install an operating system and applications software to make the computer really "happen."

It's the same with the most sophisticated e-procurement infrastructure or e-marketplace: nothing happens if you don't make it happen. And marketing is what makes stuff happen in marketplaces.

Other BAMs jumped into Net marketplaces with both feet, only to see their products' prices descending far below them. The open marketplace had commoditized them. They'd forgotten about creating value for their brands—about developing relevant differentiation for their branded products.

More picking and shoveling. More calls to Z Group, fortunately. We answered the calls with process, not magic. It's marketing based on old-fashioned P&L and income statements. It's based on writing comprehensive strategies and measuring their results. It's about managing spending for return. It's about plucking consumer dollars right out of the pockets of your competitors and putting them in your own.

THE NEW RULES AND OLD RULES MERGE: BUILDING BRANDWIDTH

As the NASDAQ plunged and anxiety rose, the argument raged: Which is going to win—the new economy or the old economy? The young Internet crowd lined up on one side of this divide and the graying BAMs on the other. As they argued, it became clear that they were both wrong. The "old" and "new" economies were headed for the same point on the horizon—the transformed economy in which new and old companies compete openly and by the same rules, many of them established several thousand years ago in the very first convenience store set up in a cave and others being clicked out today online.

In meeting rooms all over Silicon Valley and Silicon Alley and everywhere in between, Web entrepreneurs put on serious faces and promised to get back to basics—even if they'd never been anywhere near the basics in the first place.

With the excuse that the new medium demanded new rules, many Net managers had opted for NO rules. Marketing was probably the area of greatest anarchy and, as we all know by now, was the pipe down which gazillions of dollars were flushed in just a couple of years. The fact is, e or no e, marketplaces are marketplaces, and all of them are getting more crowded every day with new brands. The one thing that isn't getting rewired is the human brain; there's only so much information it can assimilate without crashing and in these jammed markets the similarity between most marketing messages and brand claims has made it even tougher to distinguish the trivial from the important.

In this crowded environment, awareness of your name or even your concept isn't nearly enough. Those few e-marketers who accepted the idea of any rules at all assumed that awareness was first among them. If you want to get awareness, take down your pants in public. Instant awareness! But does that create lasting value?

Oh, the "v" word—it used to be just the first two syllables in the really important word "valuation." **But now people realize that building value is the only way to create lasting valuation. It's value with the end user first, and valuation set by the NASDAQ analysts later, much later.**

Just as the new and old economies are merging into the transformed economy, the new and old rules of brand building are converging on a new point, which we call *building brandwidth*. **Building brandwidth means a lot more than building brand awareness. It means building brand meaning and brand power in breadth and depth, constantly adding value.** Building brandwidth requires building the brand relationship one customer at a time, one usage occasion at a time. With a lot of bumps and bruises to show for it, e-marketers have learned what most traditional marketers already know:

□ Presence in the marketplace is important, but it's not enough. Presence must be activated by visible usage and word-of-mouth testimonials in the marketplace.

☐ Customer relevance must be established and constantly replenished.

☐ Marketplace differentiation must be established and then constantly adjusted for new competitors and new claims.

☐ Brand credibility must be established in the interplay of promise and delivery, and it, too, is a constant building process.

☐ Finally, brand imagery must be defined and then added, added, added.

Building brandwidth means clearly defining who you are and where you're going. After all, as you'll hear us say again and again, if you don't define yourself, the competition will be happy to do it for you. And you won't like what they come up with—guaranteed.

Building brandwidth means developing that strong foundation of meaning described above. **It's about RELEVANCE, not awareness.** You need to develop a coherent brand architecture that relates the corporate brand, the product brands, and sub-brands. This architecture is what holds the entire brand structure together. You'll hear this again and again, too: Building brandwidth is constant. In this way it's quite unlike construction. It's more organic. It's process, not a one-time event. You no sooner celebrate the launch than you have to start shoring it up again.

THE ELEPHANT'S GRAVEYARD

Build brandwidth, and you build brand strength. Fail to build brandwidth, and you cut off the food supply for your brands. Sooner or later, they wither and die. There's an elephant's graveyard full of brands that are dead or have one foot in the hole. Consider a few examples:

Smith-Corona

Early in the spring of 2000 if you read the business pages very carefully, you learned that Smith-Corona went toes up. Web marketers might think this is just the death of natural causes of an old-economy brand. But Smith-Corona didn't have to die. The cause of death was one that a great majority of Net companies suffer from: The brand was attached to technology and attributes, not to benefits and value. Smith-Corona stood for the typewriter and typing, not for the output of typing and the value of the resulting documents.

It's a mistake we see every day on the Net: "We've got the best search engine. We've got cool technology. Our engine is faster and more robust!" Very cool. They tell you what it does, but not what it does for *you*. Given time, they'll follow old Smith-Corona right into Chapter 11. Because consumers buy benefits, not attributes. If you don't build benefits and customer value into your brandwidth, your days are numbered.

Disney

Disney obviously saw an Internet distribution outlet for all its fuzzy toys and cute clothes when it laid out multimillions of dollars for Toysmart.com. But what they'd bought was just another site where you can buy toys. And their brand positioning was the one we see most often on the Net. It's called "me, too!" That's why the Internet is awash in sameness. That's why so many sites are forgettable. And that was the death sentence for Toysmart.com. "Be different, or be damned," the late, great Roberto Goizueta of Coca-Cola said. They obviously weren't listening at Toysmart.com. Not smart. And not alive, anymore.

Campbell's

As we write this book, several deals are simmering for Campbell's, makers of Campbell's soups and . . . er . . . uh . . . there must be SOMETHING else they make, right? As those deals cook, it seems each new offer is lower than the last. Why? Campbell's provides the argument against the mantra "awareness is everything." After all, who DOESN'T know Campbell's? And who doesn't know Campbell's makes soup? Still, there's something in a brand's being *too* well known. Campbell's is soup, and when you want soup you may want Campbell's. The problem is, it seems that people just don't want canned soup as much anymore, and the marketing folks at Campbell's never added dimension to the brand, beyond chiding, "Soup is good food!" Campbell's has awareness up the ying-yang— and all of it for a category that's declining in usage. When you build brandwidth, you keep building NEW meaning on top of the old established meaning. When your brand defines the category it operates in, you have to expand the meaning of the category. New benefits, new values . . . that's building brandwidth. Fail to keep building brandwidth, and even Andy Warhol can give you *only* fifteen minutes of fame.

Boo.com
Boo.com proves how unforgiving the environment is out there today. To paraphrase F. Scott Fitzgerald, there are no second acts on the Net. In that critical first phase of building brandwidth, defining your brand, you'd better get it right and get it right the first time. Yes, developing strategic plans is tedious work. It takes time and effort and it's boring. But without that discipline on the launch pad, you end up missing Mars by about five hundred thousand miles. And you can bet nobody will even notice your absence.

WHO'LL BE NEXT?

They all ended up as "roadkill on the information superhighway," as Nathan Mhyrvold, Microsoft's former strategic compass, calls it.

Who'll be next? It will be interesting to watch the obituary pages. Who'll win the big landgrab battles of the Net? How about Amazon versus Borders? Amazon.com has built its brandwidth on customer-centricity, and they've certainly continued to expand the meaning of Amazon from books to music to toys and on and on. But have they stretched the brand meaning too thin? The advantage Borders has is certainly not yet realized—it's the integration of the Net and bricks and mortar . . . clicks and mortar, some people call it. Borders has the advantage of letting customers get what they want where and when they want it under one brand. Granted, there will be more and more Internet buyers, but will there be people who shop exclusively on the Internet? Probably only at the margins of the markets. The heaviest market activity will be among those who make planned, prompted, and impulse purchases in multiple channels. **The winning companies will be the ones who build their brand strongly in all of the channels and for all of the possible purchasing occasions. That's building brandwidth.**

WHAT'S IN IT FOR YOU?

This book is branded, naturally, and right about now you're asking the question all consumers eventually ask of any brand: "What's in it for me?"

Is this another "nice to know"? Or is it a critical "need to know"?

To answer the question, consider the role of marketing in your company. Are you interested in building value? If not, you must be a federally mandated monopoly, a company owned by the Chinese People's Army, or a complete idiot. **We take a strong view toward building value. We say it's the role of marketing. Indeed, everything your company does and says at any moment—down to the tiniest, nittiest-grittiest detail—either adds or subtracts value.** This includes you and every detail of your work; in this superheated competitive environment, there's no neutral ground. Everything you say and do is about marketing, about building up or tearing down value. Everything markets. And everybody markets—in everything they do, all employees in your organization either add or subtract value. At a fast food outlet the front-line employees play a more important role than even advertising. Ads get people to the store, but a surly employee will undo all the good will built by your ads or promotions.

So the stakes for building brandwidth, the key element of e-marketing, are high. They're just as high for online companies as for offline companies. Building brandwidth is important because it's all about all you do. Whether you work in the mail room or marketing department or manufacturing line, your job is building brandwidth. Your work will define the product (nothing communicates brandwidth louder or clearer), define the customer relationship (nothing sustains brandwidth stronger or longer), and communicate to your target audiences (otherwise you're practicing "field of dreams" marketing: "If we build it, they will come").

What's in it for you? **Building brandwidth is science, not art. You're not born with a talent for it. It takes work. It's discipline, not creative whimsy. And in this book we'll teach you the disciplines and processes of building brandwidth one customer at a time, one usage occasion at a time.**

We'll help you build brandwidth for a traditional BAM or an Internet business. In the evolving transformed economy, the ways to build brandwidth will be the same for both. And in that new environment, only the fittest brands will survive.

We'll teach you how the BAMs can maximize the value of their assets using Internet technology. Right now, the Internet strategies for most of the BAMs are about protecting assets, not building them. Building brandwidth means expanding your value across every aspect of your operations and every channel of your distribution and sales.

We'll help you understand the laws of the jungle for Web companies. There are no second chances on the Net, and no silver medal for second place. There's no more room for second-tier players in any market today. It's White House or outhouse. We'll teach you how to be the winner in today's winner-takes-all markets.

We'll reinforce the basics stressed in The End of Marketing As We Know It: *how to use marketing to sell more stuff to more people more of the time.*

Now that the NASDAQ has sobered up, you realize you can't scale the heights with sizzle—it takes skills, technology, and brand. We can't give you the skill, and you'll have to go somewhere else for the technology. But you came to the right place for building brandwidth. Building brandwidth is the key to building the customer relationship and developing its value to the max. Only when you've built a brand to its maximum depth can you begin to expand that relationship with new or extended brands in the same brand family.

Building brandwidth begins with a seminal moment in the history of e-marketing: Super Bowl 2000. The Rams weren't the only winners and the Titans the only losers that day. To find out who scored in building brandwidth, read on.

SUPERBOWL 2000: THE FIRST SUPER BOWL OF INTERNET ADVERTISING

Advertising is everybody's favorite marketing tactic. And, unfortunately, it's what many people think of as marketing itself. That's changing—but not fast enough for us. All of us watched "Dot.Com XXXIV," or the Super Bowl, as some called it. Our perspective of the game and the couple of weeks of ramp-up promotion before it and ramp-down advertising analysis after it should give you a sense of how seriously we take the craft of advertising these days. How many of those Web firms advertising during the Super Bowl were literally betting the company on the outcome of their ads?

We have developed a reputation as being tough on the ad business and its many eccentricities. If so, it's only because of the importance of this cog in the wheel of commerce. Advertising is just too important to e-marketing to be left to its own devices and vices. Super Bowl 2000 says a lot about the state of the art and science of advertising at the dawn of the new millennium. We ran a major piece of research with Penn, Schoen & Berland, the respected market and political polling firm, to measure not the ads' likeability or ridiculousness, but the purchase intent they created in viewers. The results were fairly startling.

Although the first *bona fide* techie ad spot to be aired during a Super Bowl broadcast was placed by Apple Computer during the 1984 game, the first true Super Bowl of Internet advertising didn't take the field until January 30, 2000, when fully sixteen of the game's fifty-two ad spots were placed by pure Internet companies. The sudden entrance of these high tech gamblers willing to bet the bulk of their annual marketing budgets on a single media buy drove the cost of Super Bowl ads up to $2.2 million per 30-second spot. In the last weeks before the actual broadcast, ABC was trying to buy back the spots it had originally sold to advertisers for $1.6 million in order to resell them. All this despite the fact that viewership of the NFL's premier broadcast event has been flat or declining for several years. And ABC laughed all the way to the bank, bringing in a record

$130 million in advertising revenue, a 38% increase over Super Bowl 1999.

The dot.com advertisers were betting that they could cut through the barrage of traditional Super Bowl ad pitches and reach a massive audience with a compelling message. The Super Bowl, after all, is a hundred-million-person focus group for advertising. Try to imagine a comparable event, when people sit still for the advertising and get up to go to the bathroom during the game time. Given the "gerbils shot from cannons" kind of stunts we'd seen in many Internet ads, we were skeptical that the ad agencies behind these spots could make those bets pay off. Moreover, we'd become deeply cynical about the powder-puff analysis of Super Bowl advertising that had become widely accepted by the media and business communities over the past decade. *USA Today*'s "Super Bowl ad meter" measured only ad likeability, which somehow become the de facto standard by which Super Bowl ads were judged to be successful.

But when did ad likeability become a reliable predictor of purchase behavior and business results? The answer is never. The "Mean Joe Greene" Coca-Cola spot showed that. Everybody loved it, but nobody bought anything because of it. So not only had the pricing of Super Bowl ad spots become outrageous, but the standard by which their effectiveness was judged had become disconnected from the idea of delivering tangible business results through marketing communications. How had the discipline of marketing become so lax? It was certainly frustrating to watch.

Rather than just complain about this sad state of affairs, we decided to put our money where our mouths are. We dug into our own pockets and fielded a comprehensive research study to scientifically measure the impact and effectiveness of every ad spot aired nationally during Super Bowl 2000. This would allow us to determine the true outcome of the first Super Bowl of Internet advertising.

The goal was to measure the impact of each Super Bowl ad on consumers' **purchase intent** for the product or service being advertised. Purchase intent is the most reliable predictor of actual consumer purchase behavior when all other factors, such as pricing and availability, are held equal. In addition, this is the metric that best reflects the role of advertising in the marketing mix, which is to stimulate consumers' desire for a product or service. It is the job of the remaining elements of the marketing mix to convert that desire into an actual purchase.

In the study, data were gathered on 1,450 consumers' purchase intent for each brand advertised in the Super Bowl both before and after they saw each commercial. The data were gathered through telephone interviews that were conducted during the 24 hours before the game and then again at the end of each quarter during the game to capture respondents' purchase intent shortly after they viewed each commercial. For comparison purposes, we also gathered data on the likeability of each ad.

Of course, USA Today was out gathering likeability data as well, and Monday morning after the big game found the usual suspects at the top of the paper's "ad meter" likeability rankings. Budweiser captured the top honors for the second consecutive year, followed by Pepsico's Mountain Dew spot. USA Today's lead business story that morning was that the Internet advertisers had been beaten soundly in the likeability rankings by the Super Bowl's traditional offline advertisers. This was evidenced by the fact that only one pure Internet company had cracked their top ten list. The paper was joined by other mainstream business media in declaring that the first Super Bowl of Internet advertising was decidedly "not ready for prime time."

Our research told a different story. It cast serious doubt on the effectiveness of the spots that the USA Today ad meter had rated so highly and indicated that the first Super Bowl of Internet advertising had been a much higher scoring contest when measured by purchase intent. We detail the key findings of our study here to illustrate the dichotomy between popular beliefs and scientific analysis when it comes to e-marketing and Super Bowl advertising.

Ad likeability is a poor predictor of purchase intent. When we compared our purchase intent and likeability data with the *USA Today* rankings, it was clear that ad likeability had little to do with increasing consumers' desire to purchase a product or service. Only four of *USA Today*'s top ten ads delivered statistically significant increases in purchase intent, as Table 1 shows. The remaining six generated either slight increases or significant *decreases* in purchase intent. In fact, the Mountain Dew, Motorola, and Electronic Data Systems ads delivered such negative results that they are likely doing more harm than good by being on the air at all, much less during the Super Bowl broadcast.

Some of the least likeable ads on the Super Bowl were the most effective. By the same token, some of the ads deemed least likeable by the *USA Today* ad meter and the respondents in our survey were among the most effective in increasing consumer purchase intent.

Table 1.   Likeability Rating Versus Percent Change in Purchase Intent for *USA Today*'s Top Ten Super Bowl Ads

| | | | Zmarketing | |
Ad	USA Today Ranking	Ad Age Rating	Likeability Ranking	% Change in Purchase Intent
Budweiser Beer—acting dog	1	***	7	7.8
Mountain Dew—cheetah	2	***	12	−15.0
Tropicana—running grandma	3	**ᵎ	11	25.2
Budweiser Beer—talking dog	4	***	7	−2.0
Pets.com—singing dog	5	***	24	102.1
Federal Express—Wizard of Oz	6	***ᵎ	1	6.0
Oxygen Media.com—pink baby	7	—	35	77.1
Bud Light—elevator	7	*	1	34.6
Motorola—nonvenomous snake	9	***	17	−38.9
Electronic Data Systems	10	**ᵎ	32	−28.8

In fact, the Oldsmobile ad that *USA Today* ranked dead last in like-ability delivered a whopping 67% increase in purchase intent among viewers. As Table 2 shows, fully five of the ten least likeable ads delivered significant increases in purchase intent. This is not to suggest that ad likeability and purchase intent are negatively related. After all, a number of unpopular ads created little purchase intent as well, as was the case with the ads by MicroStrategy, Lifeminders.com, and Monster.com.

Super Bowl ads that rank high on the USA Today ad meter have a poor record of real business results. We've established that *USA Today*'s ad likeability ratings don't predict purchase intent, but what about actual business results? The *USA Today* ad meter has been around for years; what kind of business results have been generated by recent Super Bowl ads ranked highly by the ad meter? We

Table 2. Likeability Ratings Versus Percent Change in Purchase Intent for *USA Today*'s Bottom Ten Super Bowl Ads

| | | | Zmarketing | |
Ad	USA Today Ranking	Ad Age Rating	Likeablity Ranking	% Change in Purchase Intent
Titan AE—feature film	38	—	31	N/A
MicroStrategy—airport man	39	*	50	−31.8
Computer.com—home film	40	★★★✓	34	24.0
Budweiser Beer—historic family biz	41	★★★	6	15.6
MicroStrategy—airport woman	42	*	41	−13.6
Hotjobs.com	43	★★★	28	−6.1
Lifeminders.com—chopsticks	44	★★	45	−8.2
Kforce.com	45	—	44	722.2
Wall Street Journal online	46	★★	39	40.7
Monster.com—city streets 2nd half	47	★★	49	−45.5
Monster.com—city streets 1st half	47	★★	43	−53.5
Oldsmobile—cars song	48	★★★✓	40	67.1

decided to investigate and found that the business results bolster our argument.

Looking back, we found that ad spots for the Pepsi brand topped *USA Today*'s ad meter rankings for the 1996 through 1998 Super Bowls. Given their success in the likeability ratings, one would presume that these Pepsi ads were aired for the remainder of the first quarter of each of these years. Further, one would expect that given Pepsi's multimillion-dollar investment in creating and airing these spots during Super Bowl broadcasts, the Pepsi brand should achieve strong business results during the first quarters of these years. Unfortunately for Pepsi, that does not appear to have happened.

According to AC Nielsen retail sales data, Pepsi-Cola brand volume growth lagged statistically significantly behind that of Coca-

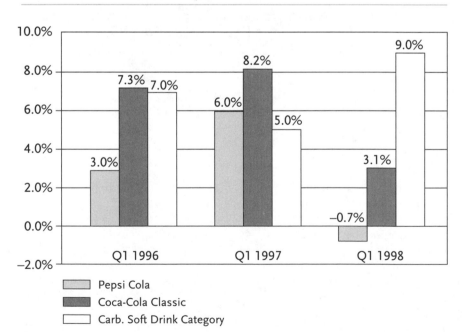

Brand Pepsi USA Volume Growth Performance
First Quarter 1996–1998

Cola Classic in the first quarters of 1996, 1997, and 1998, as shown. In fact, Pepsi's sales volume actually declined by nearly 1% in the first quarter of 1998.

Those aren't the kind of business results we'd call successful. So we've been wondering why advertisers like Pepsi keep coming back with the same likeable but ineffective ads for the Super Bowl each year. They're clearly not delivering favorable business results. Could it be that over the years these companies have figured out that the likeability formula earns them some media kudos after each Super Bowl? Would they really blow millions of dollars in Super Bowl ads for a little positive press? We hope not, but it wouldn't be the first time we've seen it happen.

Purchase intent data tell a different story. So which Super Bowl ads *were* effective in boosting consumers' intention to buy the product or service being advertised? Well, there were many effective ads, and they increased viewers' purchase intent dramatically, as Table 3 shows. In addition, fully six of the ten ads that were the most effective, on a percent increase basis, were fielded by Internet firms.

Viewers' purchase intent responses identified the Kforce.com ad as the most effective one aired during the Super Bowl, with a 72% increase in those indicating they would definitely use the website after viewing the ad. As a group, the top ten most effective ads increased viewer purchase intent by an *average of 193%!* Not too shabby. In addition, none of the top ten ranked higher than 16th in ad likeability, with most ranking 30th or lower.

Some might argue that viewers had such low purchase intent levels for the Internet companies' products beforehand that their percentage increases are somewhat misleading. Fair argument, but when you examine the data for absolute increases, the picture doesn't change much. By this measure, the Mission to Mars spot moves up from 3 to 1 in rankings, and the Gladiator, Kforce.com, BMW, and Pets.com ads all remain in the top ten. These ads were highly

Table 3. Percent Increase in Viewers' Intent to Purchase
Product or Service Advertised during Super Bowl 2000

Ad	Effectiveness Ranking	% of Viewers Who Would Definitely Use Product or Service		Before vs. After % Change
		Before Game	After Ad	
Kforce.com	1	0.9	7.4	722.2
Onmoney.com—Paper monster	2	0.9	5.5	511.1
Mission to Mars—Feature film	3	4.8	24.5	410.4
Ourbeginning.com—Fighting brides	4	0.8	3.0	275.0
John Nuveen—Christopher Reeves	5	1.0	2.8	180.0
BMW—X5 in the woods	6	3.2	8.3	159.4
Epidemic.com—Bathroom	7	1.7	4.4	158.8
Gladiator—Feature film	8	8.6	18.0	109.3
Pets.com—Singing dog	9	4.8	9.7	102.1
eTrade.com—Basketball dancers	10	4.9	9.0	83.7

effective no matter how you slice it. Nonetheless, several traditional advertisers, such as Budweiser, Visa, and Tropicana rise to the top tier on an absolute basis as a result of their extraordinarily high pre-exposure purchase intent levels, as Table 4 shows.

In addition, only two Internet advertisers remain in the top ten on this basis. But perhaps the most useful measure of marketing effectiveness for Internet firms is also among the most immediate: website traffic. So which way did the eyeballs go after the first Super Bowl of Internet advertising?

Website traffic supported purchase intent data. According to the website traffic data gathered by Media Metrix in the 24 hours immediately after the Super Bowl, many of the Internet firms that ranked highly in our purchase intent research experienced dramatic increases

Table 4. Absolute Increase in Viewers' Intent to Purchase
Product or Service Advertised during Super Bowl 2000

| Ad | Effectiveness Ranking | % of Viewers Who Would Definitely Use Product or Service | | Before Game vs. After Point Change |
		Before Game	After	
Mission to Mars—Feature film	1	4.8	24.5	19.7
Visa—Pole vault	2	42.6	58.2	15.6
Bud Light—Elevator	3	28.9	38.9	10.0
Tropicana—Running grandma	4	37.3	46.7	9.4
Gladiator—Feature film	5	8.6	18.0	9.4
Kforce.com	6	0.9	7.4	6.5
Budweiser Beer—Historic family biz	7	34.7	40.1	5.4
BMW—X5 in the woods	8	3.2	8.3	5.1
Pets.com—Singing dog	9	4.8	9.7	4.9
Oldsmobile—Cars song	10	7.0	11.7	4.7

in consumer traffic. Traffic at Kforce.com increased 2,600% directly as a result of their Super Bowl ad spot and placement, as shown in Table 5. There were losers as well: eTrade.com experienced a 5.5% decline in traffic to match the 14.3% decline in purchase intent delivered by their ad spot.

So the first Super Bowl of Internet advertising was won handily by Kforce.com, which registered dramatic gains in purchase intent and website traffic. With the kind of results that Internet advertisers generated in this year's Super Bowl advertising blitz, you can bet that even more of them will be back next year, despite the misguided criticism they received from the mainstream business press. After all, they're likely much more interested in strong business results than in a few fleeting press clippings. We can only hope that more ad agencies and advertisers follow their lead.

Table 5. Consumer Traffic after the Super Bowl

	USA Today Ranking	Ad Age Rating	Likeability Ranking	Zmarketing	
				% Change in Viewers' Purchase Intent	Media Metrix Website Traffic after Super Bowl
Kforce.com	45	—	44	722.2	2600.0
Onmoney.com—					
Paper monster	34	—	42	511.1	N/A
Ourbeginning.com—					
Fighting brides	20	*⸱	43	275.0	989.0
Epidemic.com—Bathroom	32	—	51	158.8	N/A
Pets.com—Singing dog	5	***	24	102.1	311.0
Oxygen.com—Pink baby	7	—	35	77.1	32.0
WSJ.com	46	**	39	40.7	38.0
EDS.com	10	**⸱	21	36.7	N/A
Britannica.com	33	*⸱	33	30.9	53.0
AutoTrader.com	35	***	19	26.7	414.0
Computer.com—Home film	40	***⸱	34	24.0	2502.0
Hotjobs.com	43	***	28	−6.1	240.0
Lifeminders.com—					
Chopsticks	44	**	45	−8.2	134.0
eTrade.com—Money out the					
wazoo	15	—	35	−14.3	62.5
Charles Schwab—Ringo Starr	—	***	23	−34.8	13.0
Monster.com—City streets					
1st half	47	**	43	−53.5	4.5

2

We've spent a good part of the past two years in some pretty strange places—not in the polished boardrooms of the big blue chip companies we traditionally worked for, but in slightly shabby Soho lofts, recently abandoned industrial parks, almost deserted office buildings, that born-again Pizza Hut. For much of the time, we've been doing e-marketing. We've worked with some companies that were fifteen minutes old and still slimy from the birth canal. We've worked with some people whose idea of marketing is looking in the Yellow Pages under "Advertising Agencies."

WHAT *IS* E-MARKETING?

e-Marketing is marketing online. Its purpose is to sell stuff—the same job marketing has offline. If it doesn't do that, it's not marketing at all; it's just very expensive ornamentation. e-Marketing is marketing, but it's marketing at a much faster speed, often with much higher consequences. Consider it turbo marketing. And the stakes are getting higher and higher and higher. Because more and more and more often Internet companies are being asked to do what ALL companies must eventually do: To perform. To produce revenues and profits.

This is the new marketing: results-focused, hardscrabble marketing. It's the only way to get to the mother lode. It's going to take hard work and sweat . . . digging and digging . . . even if you have to dig it out with your fingernails. And it's going to take talent and expertise; it's going to take the best that marketing has to offer. **e-Marketing is supposed to convince people to come back more often to buy more and be willing to pay more.** If you've been paying attention, you know that's the purpose of all marketing. e-Marketing, like ALL marketing, is supposed to sell stuff, and we take this business of selling stuff very seriously. Actually EVERYBODY is taking selling stuff very seriously these days. Not just selling stuff to conference rooms full of back-slapping venture capitalists, but selling stuff to real consumers, the ones who don't slap backs, don't laugh at your jokes, don't move a muscle toward your product or service unless you give them a lot of very good reasons.

Marketing has always been slow to change, even resistant to change. Little in marketing basics has changed over the past four or five decades. David Ogilvy's 1952 book, *Ogilvy on Advertsing,* for instance, remains the bible in the advertising industry almost fifty years later. But already since 1995 marketing on the Internet has gone through two important phases and has now moved into the third and most important phase.

THE FIRST PHASE OF E-MARKETING

The first phase of e-marketing was essentially no marketing at all. The Internet was the domain of avid early adopters . . . mostly propellerheads. There were just a few commercial sites, such as Yahoo!, AOL, and a little startup in Seattle called Amazon, after the river. The distribution system for e-marketing in that first phase of the Internet was the magic of discovery. This is what early adopters do in any emerging market: they seek out the best and most interesting. And there's no more effective distribution system than having your prime prospects seek you out. In this first phase brand meaning for these sites was developed in the experience of product usage and in the customer relationship and in the spontaneous conversations of these avid early users. That gave these brands their high relevance with their small groups of customers. **Differentiation was created by the simple lack of competitors in the space at that time.**

This business was defined not by the rules of marketing but by the ancient rules of merchanting (which our spell checker tells us is a made-up word—but you get the idea; what merchants have done forever in the one-to-one sale). What these companies did, the relationship they were establishing with customers, was exactly what merchants have done for thousands of years in order to convince their customers to come back more often to buy more. They were based on the simple two foundational premises of personal selling (what we call "e-merchanting"), namely, "What can I do for you?" and "What ELSE can I do for you?"

Communications were almost 100% viral in this phase of e-marketing, passed from person to person. This is the way brands off the Net have grown, as well. Think about the growth of Starbucks. And much of the growth of Disney's theme parks was without traditional marketing. When Disney decided to keep the parks open at night, for instance, the news traveled like the sounds of jungle drums. Of course, word-of-mouth advertising is the most powerful form of advertising on the planet. This is what established the early successes of the Internet. The Net may never ever again have stronger marketing. This is the essence of marketing in its most basic form. The first phase of e-marketing had no formal marketing, but virtually all aspects of its communications were market focused and highly effective as marketing communications.

THE SECOND PHASE OF E-MARKETING (1996–1999)

The second phase of e-marketing probably began when AOL adopted the mission of making their service as ubiquitous as the telephone but infinitely more useful. Their plan was that everybody in America would eventually HAVE to be using AOL, and that meant AOL would have to greatly increase penetration of both their online service and online services of every kind. In other words, they'd have to sell the category of online usage along with selling their own brand's relevance and differentiation in the category. Every pioneer brand has had to do this, whether it was Ford or Tide or McDonald's. This began AOL's push into the mass market. Their marketing strategy has been what we call a "pulse strategy"—meaning, if you didn't receive an AOL starter CD (or two, or ten), you didn't have a pulse. This is the equivalent of the old tasting booths at the supermarket. You tried it 200 times, until you finally bought it consciously, not by accident or intercept marketing. AOL borrowed from the tried-and-true sampling methods to get penetration. And penetration they got.

Priceline.com was the first major Internet player to establish their brand on the basis of fairly traditional marketing principles. Particularly effective was their fundamental Procter & Gamble–like problem/solution advertising on radio, using the remarkably astute choice of a presenter, William Shatner (totally credible to grown-ups, totally camp to young people). Early e-marketers were fairly religious about using the Internet to sell Internet services, but the rapid expansion of Internet usage made it necessary to expand beyond the target audience of current users. This was done using the most powerful concept related to the Internet, one you'll hear much more about later in the book: inevitability—"This is the way it's going to be" and "This is where you're going to be." Through the concept of inevitability you define the future as manifest destiny, one thing Bill Gates has done better than anyone in the information economy. For a decade or longer, every keynote address, every product introduction, and every interview he did consisted of defining the future on Microsoft's terms, but in so compelling a fashion that you, the listener, wanted to buy into it. Such was the usage imagery that Priceline.com developed for their brand: "This thing is gonna be big . . . REALLY BIG!" Shatner boasted.

The second phase of e-marketing was not just a marketing success story. Indeed, there were many companies that bet their entire assets on marketing and e-vaporated. This is what we call the phase of advertising with a nose ring. "Hey. We don't wear ties. We walk around in shorts. We look weird. Our advertising should look weird."

It was assumed that all Internet users were young, male (the Internet industry landscape is very male, after all), and inclined toward fraternity house humor—three strikes against this phase of e-marketing, if you ask us. It was assumed that if people laugh at the advertising, they'll decide to come to the site and use the service or buy the products. Sure! This assumption has never been borne out in reality in the history of any other kind of marketing, but these people weren't reading history; they intended to make it.

The designated marketing person at the startup, who was seldom, if ever, actually trained in the business of marketing, mind you, would no sooner get the title "VP Marketing" than he or she would dial up an ad agency. We call it "marketing without a license": it was as if a degree in marketing were instantly bestowed the moment you got second-round financing. The marketing meetings at these startups would involve everybody in the company, including the receptionist and a couple of venture capitalists for spice. All of them would be saying to themselves, "Hey, this marketing stuff isn't so hard."

For the ad agencies, this period was truly Valhalla: For fifty years, advertising creative people have been begging for complete creative freedom. Here was a group of clients begging them just to tell good jokes. Holy moley! Suddenly strange things were happening on TV sets all over the fruited plain: Gerbils were being shot out of cannons, going to the proctologist was used as a metaphor for buying computer equipment . . . monkeys and monkey humor were a particular favorite. There were hundreds more iterations of this phase of e-marketing in advertising that just simply slipped by unnoticed. When a stupid Internet ad falls in the forest, does it make a sound? Maybe, maybe not, but that distinct smell you notice is the odor of venture capital smoldering. After sitting in these meetings you come away with a sore neck from shaking your head and asking, "Where the hell is the strategy?"

This was a time when companies were still picking out nonsense names for themselves, based on coolness rather than common sense. Webforia? What is it? But the more crowded every market space got with competitors, the more important it was to provide guidance and navigation to consumers in that space.

"A hard-to-remember name will be remembered exactly because it's hard to remember," they told us. Yeah, sure.

Given the clutter and sameness on the Net, we have always recommended what we call Cup-a-Soup naming, after Lipton's venerable product: What's not to understand?? No appetizer, no sandwich, no dessert . . . it's just an INSTANT CUP OF SOUP!

It's time to tell people what you're all about and what you're going to do for them in a very quick hurry. They're not going to wait around to try to understand an obscure name.

It's fair to say the second phase of Internet marketing isn't really over. There will always be that corner of marketing that is nonsensical, undisciplined, and underachieving. It's the same offline as online. And there is a pretty strong pull to that corner of the vocation. Ad man Jerry Della Femina called advertising "the most fun you can have with your clothes on."

In e-marketing and bricks-and-mortar marketing, there will always be a lot of naked people out there, a whole lot of emperors with no clothes.

THE THIRD PHASE OF E-MARKETING

We're now entering the third and most important phase of e-marketing. After the swoon of the NASDAQ in April 2000, investment bankers and stockbrokers have gotten very serious about that little issue of revenues. "But the idea is the company will make money someday, right??" They're beginning to demand (how totally uncool!) that Internet companies actually have a business plan. A business plan must ask, "How are you going to get some business?" It's not just a bunch of financial projections. These financial backers are increasingly expecting companies to show a plan that explains how they will eventually someday sell people something at some kind of profit . . . PLEASE!! They ask about the market research that supports this plan. They even ask for a marketing plan, and not just to see the advertising, but to see the plan behind it.

The poster child for this new phase of e-marketing is CNET.com. Great company. Great site. Great business concept and plan—but with the worst marketing (and particularly the worst advertising) in the history of bad marketing. You're not likely to remember that campaign. But you may remember the article in the *Wall Street Journal* about how they had managed to virtually spend the company's total revenues on an ad campaign that failed to convince users to use CNET.com. (If that wasn't the point of the campaign, what WAS it?) This ad had a guy asking for computer advice from his proctologist, among other less memorable concepts. All this must have elicited a meeting (oh, to have been a fly on the wall at that meeting!) in which the CEO fired the agency and made the unreasonable demand that the advertising would have to work; it would have to make something happen; it would have to get results.

This may have been the catalytic moment of this newest phase of Internet marketing. You've undoubtedly seen the redesigned CNET.com campaign: people wearing T-shirts with the designations "you," "CNet," and "the right computer"—the most didactic stuff since Dick and Jane saw Spot run. This stuff follows the KISS (Keep It Simple, Stupid) rule of communications to a remarkable conclusion. It is simply brilliant. And it works; CNET.com is one of the few business-to-consumer sites that takes a licking and keeps on ticking.

WELCOME TO E-MARKETING

Now we are separating the marketing women and men from the girls and boys. Now marketing is beginning to get serious . . . and interesting. But it's also incredibly scary—after all, you've got to sell stuff and make money. Quite often, your personal wealth depends not on a guaranteed salary and bonus, but on the performance of your company for investors in the marketplace. This is high-stakes poker.

Of course, you shouldn't have to go through what CNET.com went through (like many, many million bucks or so, we'd guess) to find your way to effective e-marketing. **You must understand that the patience with living off investment dollars is over. People are going to expect you to close the sale online. You're going to have to develop revenues. If you don't do that, you're not doing**

e-marketing. You may be doing a $2 million ad on the Super Bowl, but you're not doing e-marketing if you're not doing e-selling.

That's the whole reason why we wrote this book. We continue on the same path as *The End of Marketing As We Know It*, talking about branding and teaching you how to build the most valuable asset on the Internet: brandwidth. A brand relationship is like any relationship. It can be casual and forgettable, or it can grow in breadth and depth. It can become rich and lasting for both sides of the relationship. That's what happens with the best brands on and off the Net. That's what building brandwidth is all about. It really can't be attained without achieving the sale, without closing. Brandwidth assumes that product usage, the most important communicator of brand meaning, will be developed along with all other aspects of brand building.

The rules of e-marketing that you'll read in this book are pretty simple, but very solid. Follow them, and you'll lead your market. As we once yelled at Steve Ballmer of Microsoft many years ago in a meeting in which he had done more than his share of yelling at us, "You guys don't have to invent marketing . . . just adopt it."

3

E-MARKETING MUST BE E-FFECTIVE

This, of course, could have been the name of every chapter in this book. And *The End of Marketing As We Know It* already filled a pretty good-sized book on the same subject: Marketing is serious business, defined by serious business principles. Marketing must sell; it must work; it must get results. **Anything that doesn't get results isn't really marketing, it's B.S. . . . and very expensive B.S.**

There are more websites than there are people in England, France, Germany, and Spain combined. The Web is crowded elbow to elbow with consumers who are trained to believe that infinite choices are only a URL or two away. One click, and you're toast. Internet investors, some of the most patient investors in the history of capitalism (willing to wait five years for profits, in many cases), are beginning to show signs of unrest: they're taking a hard look at the burn rate of Internet startups—the rate at which they spend money, particularly on marketing activities—and demanding to know just how and when revenue is going to overtake spending. "Show me the money!"

They're using the "r" word a lot more often, the word that was unheard of early in the history of the Net: RESULTS. Can you or can you NOT close the sale online? B2C (business-to-consumer) e-marketing has established itself principally on one tactic: FREE!!! "Come use our Net service . . . for FREE!!!" and "Download our software . . . totally FREE!!!" Whoever said there is no free lunch? You can eat it on the Internet. And there are even Web companies that will PAY you to eat that free lunch. Who knew?!

Again and again, we read that a Net company is overhauling its business plan because of a recurrent situation: lots of traffic but no transactions and a lot of investors getting testy about it.

This value system of B2C e-commerce dooms profitability from the start. Customers who were attracted to B2C sites with free services are proving recalcitrant to being charged for these services. Imagine!

So marketing in the new economy is having to sober up in a hurry. Advertising that was meant to entertain and amuse is now expected to sell, and sell again. Son of a gun! PR that was meant to develop an edgy, youthful image for the company is now meant to mature that image in a hurry. Ouch! "I work at a dot.com" is no longer an excuse for nonperformance. In fact, "I work in marketing at McDonald's" or "I work in marketing at Nike" or "I work in marketing at Levi's" used to spare you from the harsh judgment of results. No more. Marketing isn't to make happy, it's to make money. And that's the cry in category after category, from banks to bagels. Marketing on the Net is no different from marketing off the Net in this way. If anything, it's a tougher marketing situation online.

The Net is all about marketing. If the Net is going to work, its marketing is going to have to work.

So e-marketing must be e-ffective. It must target, reach, engage, hold, sustain interest, and promote usage and encourage loyalty. e-Marketing must close the sale with customers and often at the same time sell the company itself to investors and analysts.

GOD IS IN THE DETAILS

In developing political strategy, we learned an important lesson and have the scar tissue to prove it: **Everything communicates.** Every detail of a campaign—everything that candidates and their helpers say or do and sometimes what they fail to say or do— communicates to some important constituency. In our corporate consulting, we found that the corollary applies. Everything markets. And we mean everything. Every aspect of operations and communications is important. God is in the details. When you ask what sells Coca-Cola, for example, ask yourself these questions:

- ☐ Is it the remarkable, refreshing product?
- ☐ Is it the package? The bottle or can or twelve-pack carton?
- ☐ Is it the pricing?
- ☐ Is it the distribution of the product and its positioning on the shelf in the store, or behind the counter at the diner?
- ☐ Is it the in-store promotion or merchandising?
- ☐ Is it advertising or PR about the company or product?
- ☐ Is it the way the trucks look on the city streets?
- ☐ Is it the way people answer the phones at the bottling company?
- ☐ Is it the way the crew kids at McDonald's pass it over the counter?

The answer is yes. It's all of that.

Think about your company, be it a dot.com or BAM (bricks and mortar). Are you telling people in every detail of your communications why they should buy your brand? Is the name meaningful to them? What about the packaging, merchandising, pricing, promotion, etcetera, etcetera? Is the phone at headquarters answered in a way that's going to help sell your product?

As we learned that every detail is important in marketing, we also learned that very few of those details are neutral. **Every detail is**

either adding value or subtracting it, selling or unselling. The effect is magnified on the Internet, where the details of selling and merchandising are literally in your face. The details of the site, and the relationship they establish with consumers, will be the most important aspects of building the brand and building brandwidth with consumers.

HOW DID IT HAPPEN?

In that first phase of e-marketing, in which some of the best-known brands on the Internet were established—Yahoo!, Excite, AOL, and Netscape—little formal planning went into marketing. Still, marketing and selling fundamentals permeated the space. **The focus then was on the two key components of e-marketing today— brand and customer.**

Brandwidth was built the old-fashioned way, developed in the customer's experience with the product, layer after layer, based on usage. Because there were radically fewer choices on the Net than there are today, these early Web brands enjoyed more of their customers' attention and time. These customers were early adopters—savvy about technology, patient with developmental bugs, curious as hell. "Tell me how to do more with your site."

Imagine a retail customer asking, "Tell me how to get deeper into your store."

HOW DO YOU MEASURE SUCCESS?

Increasing usage is the surest way to build brand loyalty. We've sat through dozens of ad agency presentations in which fashionably dressed young men and women assuredly assert that their advertising is going to make people like the brand, which will make them use the product. In these meetings you hear about things like the "aspirational brand pitch," which supposedly means allowing consumers to project through the brand all the things they can be. In the ski industry, in which we've done a lot of work, they do a great job of the "aspirational brand pitch," showing skiers diving off cliffs into the void, doing 360s, whipping past trees in a shadowy forest. Awesome! This has a terrific aspirational effect on parents from Omaha who were hoping to survive spring break with the kids: They aspire to go to the beach. All they want is a good experience with the kids. No broken anything. No jumping off cliffs. No aspiration.

The upshot is, communicate to your customers' attitudes, not your own. Adopt THEIR context and perceptions, not yours. Explain in plain language how you appeal to what they want. People are looking for guidance and navigation from marketing, but they're not going to follow that guidance off a cliff.

The early Web companies understood the unique relationship they would have with their customers. All of marketing is meant to be interactive. Theirs really achieved it. It said, "Let me tell you something about myself. Then tell me what you think. Then try using it. Here, let me help you use it. I can make it easier for you and more personal for you . . . see? Now, let me tell you more." On and on it went.

The free market is a democratic place, and democracy is dialogue: Politicians and political concepts are communicated to the electorate, and the electorate responds at the voting booth. Increasingly, that dialogue is being extended through political research, because politicians like to know the quality of their dialogue with their constituents long before the voting booth tells them.

In politics, polling concentrates on people's intent to vote in a certain way—what ideas about the candidate or issues in the campaign may influence that vote and how strongly voters feel (after all, two-thirds of U.S. voters may know who they like in any given election, but they don't like them enough to actually show up and vote). Polling helps guide the candidate in that dialogue with the people. It is constant, often conducted daily throughout the campaign, and as new information enters the environment, the dialogue shifts with it. You can tell which candidates have good and bad polling from the things they say. "Where the hell did he come up with THAT?" means the pollsters failed to connect to your concerns and beliefs about what the election is all about.

President Clinton has been not so much a political leader as the world's most astute political follower. Having lost touch with the electorate in his first term as governor in Arkansas, with the result that he was not reelected, Clinton began to listen hard to the preaching of the pollster Dick Morris. He has now totally mastered management of the hot buttons. In 1996, having lost the House and Senate elections to the Republicans and almost losing his mandate to lead, Clinton turned again to pollsters, this time Mark Penn and Doug Schoen of Penn, Schoen & Berland. They found that the Democratic brand had come to mean old-fashioned, out of touch, big government, minorities and special interests, "not for me." A brand can't get much worse off than that. Penn and Schoen began developing polling relentlessly to find the issues that might pull the Democratic brand back into relevance. After a lot of work, they found four—education, environment, Medicare, and Medicaid.

While the Republicans' fiscal and social conservatism had much better captured the imagination of the American people over the past decade, there was a tendency to believe that the Republican ideologues were overzealous (and this was *before* the impeachment mess). Those four issues—education, environment, Medicare, and Medicaid—were considered sacrosanct by a great majority of the voters, and in one way or another, Republicans had recommended cutting spending on every one of them (usually for commonsense reasons, but politics is not often about common sense; it's about perceptions).

Bill Clinton and Al Gore marched across the country and boomed over the airwaves: "We won't let those Republicans in the Congress cut education, environment, Medicare and Medicaid."

These four issues not only made the Democrats more relevant, but increased their appeal to a majority of Americans again for the first time in years. **You'd have to rate this one of the all-time best brand repositionings in history. This established the foundation for Democrats' eventual control of the congressional majority and for Clinton's big win in 1996.**

At the same time, the polls have begun to show a new phenomenon: "Clinton fatigue." No matter how deft President Clinton has become at following the electorate, the people still expect a leader to lead. And the candidate or political leader must lead the dialogue with voters—introducing ideas, providing a vision for the future, challenging ideas and attitudes of the past. The vote in marketing terms is the transaction. And it's a daily dialogue.

What does all this have to do with building brandwidth in your marketplace? Everything. **Building brandwidth is about connecting what is relevant to people to the benefits in your product or service. Building brandwidth means making that connection deeper and wider over time.** Marketers, like politicians, have tried to make that dialogue more active through research and more personal through customized marketing and customer relationship management programs. The Internet allows that conversation to take place in real time. The Internet brings back to marketing the dynamics of the face-to-face sell (it's always been a part of merchanting). The e-marketing dialogue is a rich selling environment: You sell, listen, adjust, sell better, listen, adjust, sell more intuitively what the customers need (based on what they've told you and how they've behaved in the past), listen, adjust, sell better, and sell more. Because of the speed of information transfer and the clutter of competition today, all companies, BAM and Web alike, face the same challenge: if you're not building your brand constantly, it's deteriorating constantly. Swim or die.

The early Web companies focused their marketing skills on selling themselves to investors—first to the individual angel investors, then to the venture capitalists, then to investment banks, and eventually to brokers and institutional and individual investors. The IPO "road show," so called because the management of Internet startups dress in business suits for the first time in years, get on airplanes and fly all over the country seeking investors, holding their future in their laptop—the equivalent of taking a show on the road in the old days of vaudeville—is the basic marketing document of the age. Generally it amounts to a PowerPoint presentation explaining the company, its vision, its business concept and strategy, and its management and is almost purely a marketing show—with a touch of P&L thrown in for tone.

Internet analysts, absolutely overrun by dot.com opportunity, dot.com statistics, and sell coming out of their ears and other orifices, have sustained severe damage to the attention-span parts of their brains, so these presentations must be incisive marketing communications. The "sell" must be delivered in the first three to six slides (though this doesn't keep most managers from wasting these slides on telling the analysts everything they already know about the size of the market for the Internet—you can sit there and watch the analysts' eyes glassing over as these slides click by). It's true that the earlier Web startups had the same advantage with investors that they had with customers. These first-phase investors were also early adopters—Net savvy, sold on the opportunity, curious about new developments. That's certainly not the case today. The herding mentality has had investment companies of every size and shape trying to get into the Net. Nobody wants to be left behind. And, even after the debacle of last spring, you can hear "IPO" within 15 minutes of any conversation about almost anything these days. This expansion of interest, the expanding penetration of the Net and the gold rush mentality of a horde of Internet entrepreneurs have led to an avalanche of activity in Web finance. Now it's harder and harder to get the attention of the best investors. e-Marketing is more important than ever.

HOW DO YOU SPOT SUCCESS?

The successful Internet startup is the successful marketing organization. That's not to diminish the role of the technology, but the technology is the enabling infrastructure for the marketing of service, product, and customer relationship. And in most markets technology quickly becomes a commodity. It's true in B2C and it's just as true in business to business, despite the more granular services offered.

During the second phase of e-marketing, marketing directors, ad agencies, and PR companies were hired. Shortly thereafter, e-marketing, which had been highly effective in its first phase, went off the tracks. It was an amazing process.

It was assumed early on that the Internet would revolutionize advertising and media, since it would make obsolete the mass media and the ad industry that feeds off it. The ad agencies were desperate to remain relevant. Every one of the big ad conglomerates established an Internet, online, or interactive division and found a guy with a ponytail to run it. The division was empowered to develop the totally new concepts of Web advertising. And the radical, outside-the-box concept they came up with was . . . billboards. It was *Back to the Future* . . . all the way back to the brave new world of Burma Shave.

Of course, the economic reality of the big agencies is that by and large they are not really making money unless they are placing or producing network television advertising. Agencies are high-cost operations. They have to pay for the fancy offices, burled conference rooms, and buff young people everywhere. Importantly, advertising agencies provide a community for creative people and this, too, is expensive, but it's important to the business function. All of this conspires to make it necessary for ad agencies to depend on their highest-margin services: not marketing planning or media programming, but network television. The two industries—advertising and commercial broadcast TV—are copacetic and totally dependent on each other. If you're a company with a marketing problem, the agencies' answer for fifty years, no matter what the problem, has been network television advertising. Sales down? Network TV ads. Product problems? Network TV ads. You name the problem—network TV ads have been the answer. The irony is that the more companies that bought this line of thinking, the more crowded the TV space became, chipping away at the memorability of the early advertisers. By the late 1980s you could see the effect of network television advertising waning and it was a dark time for agencies and the networks alike. That was the end of marketing as we knew it.

The agencies' movement to their Net ventures at that time was mostly tentative and defensive, intended as a way to remain relevant with their own clients, who were intrigued about the possibilities of this new distribution source for information and products. They had no idea how they were going to make money on Internet advertising.

As we've said earlier, it was AOL, when it was known more as an online service than as an ISP (Internet service provider), that pioneered e-marketing beyond the Net. And this led the way for the advertising business's current Internet boom. AOL's quest was to grab customers, but they didn't rely on the pull tactics of selling their service's relevant attributes and competitive differentiation; they threw themselves into the push marketing tactics of building, or more specifically buying, distribution. This is what Seth Godin, author of *Permission Marketing,* calls "interruptive marketing." Over the past three or four years, you couldn't open a magazine, unwrap your Sunday newspaper, or swing a dead cat without hitting an AOL starter CD.

Steve Case clearly understood the stakes of e-marketing. In five years, there wouldn't be ten or twelve big Net portals: there would be two or three. He understood the way all markets had been changing as choices increased and marketing information flooded into them. The changes were as true for Internet portals as for soft drinks or sneakers or publishers or investment banks.

Traditionally, most markets had been divided into three tiers. At the top were the well-known, well-respected, and ubiquitous brands. There were generally two or three of these brand giants in any market, be it aircraft manufacturers or athletic supporters. These market leaders sold their category's relevance to consumers in the mass market. After all, they would dominate any category growth.

Just below them was a second tier of about ten brands that benefited from the category selling done by the top tier. These brands slipstreamed the leaders like a NASCAR racer, riding in the wake of the marketing power of the category brand leaders. They tried to look and act like the big guys; they had the style, if not the impact.

Then there was the third, bottom tier of most markets, traditionally dominated by smaller, more individualistic or niche-appeal brands, regional brands, and price brands. There could be scores of these brands in any market.

The information economy has crushed this traditional architecture of markets. As consumers became aware of more and more choices and as new products continued to enter every tier of the marketplace, competition intensified. In a state of information overload, weary consumers looked for ways to streamline choice. They moved in two directions: to the top of the market, for the sure-thing brand choice (one or two at the most), and to the bottom, for niche choices to suit particular needs. The middle market is disappearing, pulverized by the brand marketing dominance of the market leaders and the personalization of niche brands at the bottom of the market. Take a minute to picture this collapse of the middle market. Use any market as an example and think about its three tiers. What's happened to the brands in that middle tier? There aren't many left.

Clearly, if you want to play at the top of the market, you have to play high-stakes poker. And nobody has done that with more commitment or cool intent than Case. He knew he'd have to play that game off the Net, essentially at the mouth of the promised pipeline of Internet growth, to win customers just as they entered the category or even BEFORE they entered it. His push marketing strategy has been dominated by sampling programs, giving the stuff away for free, a time-tested tactic in every category, as we said. That has meant buying distribution with very heavy promotion. Although AOL did little advertising during this push (they've recently begun television advertising for their AOL 5.0 release), they must have given hope to the advertising business with their heavy offline push to get online users.

It was another Net pioneer we've mentioned, Priceline.com, that actually showed the way for advertising agencies. Their reverse auction system (and its proprietary technology) allows consumers to bid for the unused inventory of airlines, hotels, car rental companies, and so on. Unlike traditional auctions, which carry with them the "winner's curse"—if you're the winning bid, you're also the highest bid—a reverse auction allows you to make a low bid and let the sellers see if they can match it. It's a cool product and business model.

And Priceline.com was the first Net brand that began building its brandwidth off the Internet (yes, AOL built its brand off the Net, but also BEFORE the Net, selling as an online service). Unlike the Web pioneers, Priceline advertised virtually from the beginning of its service. **Unlike the irreverent, obscure advertising of most Net**

**companies, Priceline's radio campaign was simple and straightfor-
ward—a classic of the genre of product introductory advertising.**
What would you say if I told you you could bid any price you want
for an airline ticket? Or to be able to sit down and play a piano? Or
to be able to get whiter whites and bluer blues? Or to be able to see
the USA in a Chevrolet? Like many Internet concepts, Priceline's
reverse auction was a new kind of shopping for most Americans.
Unlike many of its peers on the Web, though, Priceline took the
time to carefully explain the concept, using Captain Kirk to guide
consumers through it. As we've said before, this advertising also
captured the most powerful emotional motivation that exists on the
Internet: inevitability, the manifest destiny of a business idea to succeed and become a part of your life. It has been powerful advertising; judging from the results, we'd have to call it the most successful
advertising campaign in the short history of the Net.

COMPRESSION OF THE CYCLE
OF NEWNESS

As we've said, early in the development of Web companies, marketing was put on hold while the managers grandstanded their way
around the country, raising money, selling the company before they
started to sell the product.

These days e-marketing can't wait. Companies can't put their
marketing and branding on a back burner without having it go cold
and moldy. The easy, open access of the Internet is one of its
strongest attributes. This same open access has made Internet sites
vulnerable to hacker attack, however, and the transparency of Internet businesses has made corporate espionage virtually unnecessary.
Any strategic advantage introduced into the market is straightaway
seen, analyzed, and cloned.

This represents an accordianlike compression of what we call "the cycle of newness." The cycle of newness is the amount of time a new idea has to itself in the marketplace before it is copied or bettered by a competitor. Not many years ago, a new attribute in a product might enjoy 9 months to a year of clear sailing. It often took a while for competitors to realize the product had been introduced, analyze the effect of its introduction, decide to react, and formulate their reaction. That 9 months became 4 months, then 13 weeks, then 60 days, then 30. Now it's a matter of a few days or several hours. All of our Net clients scan the competition's sites constantly, looking for signs of a change in business strategy, technological capacity, or marketing tactics and ready to change their own approach immediately in reaction. If they don't change, they become market followers and get old fast. "What happened?"

You fell asleep at the wheel is what happened.

Consumers, trained by the pace of change on the Web, have transferred their Net behavior and expectations to BAM companies. Day after day we read in the *Wall Street Journal* that yet another of the companies with traditionally steady earnings is going to miss its profit target. We've seen it with Mattel, Procter & Gamble, and Coke, and we'll see it again and again and again, until they rethink their business in terms of a whole new class of consumers and consumer behavior: **Web consumerism.**

Two example events in the BAM world, both considered corporate crises, helped shorten the time between market action and reaction. The bad thing about crises is that they upset the norm. The good thing about crises is that they upset the norm. They force you to think outside the ordinary.

One was the Tylenol poisoning scare in 1983. When a crazed individual, bent on revenge, poisoned the product in several bottles of Tylenol, the result was national news. Johnson & Johnson, Tylenol's corporate parent, famously leapt into action, recalling the product nationwide before the perpetrator had even been identified, before the proof of the poison was even established. Most marketers remember that rapid response. Many forget the equally rapid development of tamper-proof packaging for the return of Tylenol to the market shelves. This changed packaging not only for Tylenol and its category of pharmaceutical competitors, but for virtually every food or medical product sold anywhere to anyone.

The second was the Coca-Cola Company's turnaround after the failed introduction of New Coke in 1985. Seventy-seven days after the heralded debut of the new product, Classic Coke had been returned to market and Donald Keough, the company's president, was on the air with a corporate statement that had never before been heard on prime-time TV: "We made a mistake." As amazing as the speed of the return was the boldness of the move, ignoring corporate pride and setting a precedent for response to corporate market crisis: "Tell the truth, tell it all, tell it fast."

On the Net, everything is considered a corporate crisis. And with good reason. The Web is an asteroid field of calamities, just waiting for you to fly into it. So response times have to be even faster than in these two famous "best practice" case histories. You have to respond to trouble before it happens.

With the life expectancy of a fruit fly, a new strategic advantage must do a lot of living quickly. It must be drained of every possible opportunity for market gain. Marketing has to get traction more quickly than ever before. There's no time for getting cute or going fuzzy. It's got to work early and keep on working. No longer can anybody afford one of those wink-wink ad campaigns typical of the second phase of Web marketing, seemingly aimed at consumers but actually targeting the mostly young, mostly male audience of Wall Street analysts and investors.

"THE BATTLE MUST BE WON BEFORE IT IS FOUGHT"

In this era of 360-degree competitive threat, your marketing gets results or gets flattened. e-Marketing is not magic. It's science, as exact as digital technology. It is meant to achieve measurable, meaningful results. So it's the end of the second phase of e-marketing, the age of absurdity. The magic show is over. It's time to go to work.

e-Marketing is marketing, plain and simple—and sometimes complex and hard, too. It's the fundamental strategies and tactics that have described the best marketing efforts for a long, long time.

Practicing e-marketing means developing a marketing and branding strategy that delivers on the needs for market presence, consumer relevance, competitive differentiation, brand credibility, and user, usage, product and associative imagery—the basics of brandwidth. This means uniting every detail of operations, communications, and interactions around a core marketing strategy. You must coordinate the efforts of internal communications, event planning and sponsorships, investor relations, community activities, public relations, advertising, merchandising, distribution, sales, customer support and customer relationship development, promotions, and corporate recruiting into one integrated whole.

Nobody may ever again get the opportunity CNET.com had to turn around its failed marketing tactics: From the beginning you'd better be ready to kick ass and take names. Your market targets must be precisely defined from the get-go: Nobody can afford shotgun blasts in Net marketing anymore. You must know in advance what will move the perceptions, attitudes, and purchase or usage behavior of your core targets. "The battle must be won before it is fought," the military strategist Sun Tzu reminds us.

The period of exploration and experimentation in e-commerce is over. The attempt to reinvent marketing has failed. It's simply time to adopt the basics of marketing and branding. Sure, a couple of billion in seed money has been flushed in the meantime, but, what the hell, it was flushed into the roiling effluence of a booming national economy, where it may serve as fertilizer for more growth and opportunity to be harvested sooner or later on the Net. So it's time to get down to the brass tacks of e-marketing and building brandwidth. It's the end of "set it and forget it" marketing plans. It means strategic dodging and weaving when necessary. It's time to get busy. It's time to make something happen.

How will you do that?

1 **You're going to the basics FIRST, instead of "back to basics."** Have you noticed? This is the topic of 99.9% of all business magazine articles featuring a corporation or corporate manager that's come back from the dead: "They got back to basics." The basics are SELLING and MAKING MONEY. Is anything more basic than that? You've got to close the sale online.

2 You'll take the gloves off—it's bare knuckles from the time you come out of your corner.

3 You won't waste time and effort talking about what your product or service can do—you'll make sure you always focus communications on the defined consumer benefit, on "what it will do for YOU, Ms. Net Shopper."

4 You'll drive differentiation into every detail of your site, service, support, and everything else. You'll develop your strategic differentiation into your brand architecture, into the naming of your products, and into the way you link together the brands in your family.

5 You won't let one single customer slip through your fingers for lack of support or the customized, personalized brand relationship you build around that person's needs and desires.

6 You'll drive your basic brand story—the "elevator story" it's called, because the whole story can be yelled into an elevator as

the doors are closing—into every kind of communication from your company and any of its brands.

7 You'll be doing all of the above at the same time you're racking up the frequent flyer miles, schlepping around the country trying to sell the whole enterprise to the most skeptical audience you'll ever have to sell.

There's plenty of money to be made on the Internet, even though the stratospheric valuations and the stock options attached to them have come fluttering down to earth. There are still gazillions to be made. But the easy Internet money is long gone. There will still be the big rewards to the winners, but we're going to have to win in much more crowded competitions, facing off against much more savvy and savage competitors and wooing a consumer market with their minds increasingly overstuffed and their attitudes increasingly cynical. From now on in e-marketing, we're all going to make money the old-fashioned way. This is your playbook for the bruising game that's being played by the new rules of e-marketing. If you bought this book, you've already started on the right track.

e-Lessons:

☐ If you read *The End of Marketing As We Know It,* you already get this point. At the end of the day, the premise underlying e-marketing is really quite old-fashioned: Understand what's important to your customers—then drive that meaning into your products and services and everything you do and say. Understand their attitudes, their language, and their sense of the competitive set in your marketplace. Learn to talk back to them in that same language, so you can sell them more stuff more often and make more money—so you can do marketing the way it's supposed to be done.

☐ In our experience, there isn't any great divide between the traditional BAMs in their marketing and the e-companies in theirs. Everyone has the same opportunities on the Web; everyone is given the same basic set of tools. The question is, what will you make with them?

☐ Because consumers keep getting smarter, you must market smarter.

☐ Because competition keeps getting tougher, you must market tougher.

☐ What you're going to read about in this book are marketing concepts you've probably heard about for years but may not have practiced. The situation, in Abraham Lincoln's words, is "piled high with difficulty." But you can rise to the occasion; it's piled equally high with opportunity. Just add e-marketing.

4

YOUR MOST IMPORTANT JOB
IS TO BUILD BRANDWIDTH

Your brand will be the most valuable asset you ever build in your company. Nothing else will come close. So you must learn to develop brandwidth. When you effectively build brandwidth with your key constituencies, your brand defines you, carrying a ton of meaning in a fraction of a second. It helps connect you to customers and prospects in the marketplace. It helps enhance the value of every transaction, allowing you to charge a premium price for your branded products and services. **Brandwidth is more important than bandwidth. No question about it.**

Brandwidth isn't just a cute name. It's the way brands have to be built in e-marketing: layer after layer of meaning connected to specific audiences, in an ever deepening connection. **High brandwidth will beat low brandwidth every time.** Coke has an industry-dominating asset in its worldwide distribution system. The product is accessible to all, and the great Robert Woodruff's mission as founder has been accomplished, putting Coke "within an arm's length of desire." The pipeline of distribution has been built. But it's brandwidth that turns it on. That's how the company grew the business on this solid base from 9 billion to 15 billion cases between 1993 and 1997. That's a lot of bubbles.

As we all know, great brands are made, not born. Few brands have had the corporate pedigree of Ford's Edsel, New Coke, McDonald's Arch Deluxe, and Microsoft's Bob. But where are they now? Genetics got them nowhere; they never survived.

Brandwidth is built with sweat, discipline, and innovation aplenty. And all the best brands have been built from the ground up.

For years, our consulting business was defined by a core principle: Every client's problem is unique, requiring a unique solution. That's just plain not true anymore. Increasingly, the problems we see with a variety of clients online and offline are quite common. In fact, they're exactly the same. In various languages, all of our clients today talk about the same thing: BRAND. The brand, they realize, is like a CD that holds for consumers all the meaning of everything the company, the products, and the customer relationship amount to and stand for.

Of course, this was true of brands fifty years ago. The definition hasn't changed. A brand is still a brand. It's just accelerated to Mach 2. And today brand building is both more difficult and more important. Branding has become part of everyday language, not just arcane marketing discussions. Political candidates talk about brands. CEOs and CFOs brag about them. Investment bankers understand how to value them. Ad agencies, sales managers, manufacturers, financiers, doctors, lawyers, and Indian chiefs (the ones who control high-rolling casinos, particularly) are all talking about brands and branding. Tom Peters, David Andrusra, and Rick Haskins write about how to brand yourself: "the brand of me."

Branding is not just another passing business fashion: It's a fact of life in the information age. It's a necessity born of the competitive noise and increasing clutter in every market environment. Brand is the shorthand of our time, instantly communicating the total idea of your product or service to a vast audience, yet conveying personal meaning to every single one of them at the same time. The competitive decibel level in every market has increased radically in just these past five years. Take a look at your supermarket's shelves. In fact, take a look at your supermarket, which has had to expand into a megamarket just to contain those overstuffed shelves.

This increase in competition is a direct result of marketers' increasing ability to get information into and out of markets more quickly and reliably than ever. Market intelligence gathering has sophisticated to the point that it is often possible to respond to product or marketing initiatives even before they go to market. This isn't corporations playing at being Bond, but corporate swagger by the marketers. Advertising, PR, and promotional agencies are famous for premature ejaculation of new market initiatives. Just read those agencies' press releases in *Ad Age* or *Brand Week*, and you'll see most big marketers' plans months before they are executed in market: "Dewey, Cheatem & Howe Designs Boffo Box Top Sweepstakes for Cheerlos." So Post, Kellogg's, and Ralston have only to buy the trade magazines to know what General Mills is doing three or four months before the program even starts. Just to level the playing field, though, the agencies working for Post, Kellogg's, and Ralston do the same thing.

One way or another, marketers of every kind almost instantly get information on consumers' perceptions, attitudes, and behavior. A new brand or a brand extension can be launched in a fraction of the time it took only a decade ago, and on the Net, e-marketers get that information instantly.

This is what has collapsed the cycle of newness, or the rate at which companies "see" and "raise" one another's strategic differentiations. These competitive "see you/raise you"s go on hour by hour on the Net. For the consumer, the result is a dizzying cycle of new products, new ideas, and new line extensions of existing products. It's also a horizon-to-horizon sea of sameness out there.

What is the difference between techies.com and monster.com? Tough to explain. And the more job boards appear, the more the consumer is confused. Of all the brand positionings we see, the one we see most is "me, too!" **There's a hell of a lot more "see you" than "raise you" in every market, online or offline.**

People are besieged by information from all sides. Since the dawn of civilization, people have sought information about the world around them. Knowing more was considered a matter of personal and emotional security. Now, perhaps for the first time in all history, people tell researchers they'd feel more secure with LESS information, not more. HELP! **To slice through this clutter is the job of branding today: The higher the brandwidth, the more likely the brand is to cut through. Low brandwidth means you get lost in the static. Sameness kills brandwidth.**

As the net expands and Web use grows, it will be harder and harder to build brands and brandwidth. The Net has already had to build brands beyond its base of early adopters, as we've already discussed. Every market has its own forward-edge group leading it. They are consumer pioneers, seeking out new concepts and leading others to them. In almost all markets, these early adopters are not motivated by traditional marketing tactics. Indeed in some markets, traditional marketing backfires with early adopters.

For example, early adopters have made the third tier of the beer market, the microbrews and craft brews, the most dynamic segment of this market (while the greatest volume remains at the top tier, with Budweiser and Bud Light, and that middle tier, once the profitable territory of Miller, Coors, Pabst, Old Style, Stroh's and others, is disappearing in the crush from above and below). The craft brews have little or no classic marketing or promotion. Early adopters in the beer market find new microbrews and mini-brews precisely because they are looking for them. They seek out the next new thing, and others follow them. Microsoft has developed all of its marketing strategies with a focus on what they call the "influential end users," the early adopters in high tech. The most powerful brand communications for the early adopters in the beer market are beer labels. Word of mouth propels the initial success of brands favored by the early adopters. It's called "viral marketing," for the speed with which the brand communications spread from person to person. But viral marketing isn't a freak of nature—it happens because of a strategy designed to create it. It's about getting out ahead of what consumers are thinking.

Ironically, when these little breweries work up the marketing resources to launch advertising, the early adopters bolt. To them, if the brand is doing advertising, it's reaching everybody everywhere. In early adopter terms, it's over. The irony of these little beer brands is that they grow to success without advertising and as soon as they begin to advertise, they decline in popularity.

Internet usage has extended far beyond that core group of early adopters now. Their business influence and viral marketing influence are much diminished. And as clutter and competition have increased, it has been harder to depend on discovery for brand trial. Many marketers have been forced to promote offline to seek trial and consideration online. In fact, Web advertising has revived the fortunes of broadcast television. In the last Super Bowl, more than a dozen of the advertisers who shelled out more than $1.5 million each to ABC for 30-second spots aimed at less than 10% of U.S. households. That gives you an idea of the stakes being waged on every Internet user today.

It turns out that developing awareness for relatively unknown Net brands is something the mass media are actually pretty good at doing. Though most of the "new" Internet commercial concepts are based on very old ideas—eBay.com as an auction, Priceline.com as a consumer RFP (request for price), and CNET.com and Deja.com as advice over the backyard fence—they often take some explaining to large audiences. Using off-line mass media to do it makes some sense. This means using broad media to reach a narrow audience of interest. Indeed, some of the Super Bowl Internet advertisers were probably very happy to reach an audience of two or three hundred analysts.

As we've said, brand naming on the Net at first derived from the unconventional attitudes of its young developers. The story goes that Yahoo! took their name from the response of the first bankers they approached for financing: "Do you really expect us to lend money to a couple of yahoos like you?" The more absurd the name, the more memorable it would be, they assumed. This may in fact have been true in the market of Internet early adopters, just as it is true of microbrew early adopters. Naming is often an inside joke among these first movers. But now absurd names have become clutter themselves. There are simply too many to remember. For company or product/service brand names, we strongly suggest the "Cup-a-Soup" example. That's the sensible place to start development. If you find one that's not taken, that's the sensible place to end it, too.

Consumer attention span is decreasing on the Net as it did earlier at the supermarket. Loblaw's, the giant Canadian food retailer, has been reported to say that today 80% of its customers' brand decisions are made at the shelf in 6 seconds or less. On the Net, it's been estimated that the average hit time for any given site is maybe half that. The consumer masses aren't as brand adventurous as the early adopters. They don't have time to be. In all categories, they are making brand decisions closer and closer to the point of sale—ever heightening the value of effective communications in that area, and this is as true on the Net as it is in the retail store. In other words, the point of decision keeps moving closer to the point of sale. On the Net, it's most often the same place.

On the Net, the key issue at the point of decision is easy to identify but hard to deliver: stickiness. What will keep customers around longer, in order to get more usage, more satisfaction, more sales, and the likelihood of more brand loyalty? The huge gap between a hit or visit and an actual e-commerce transaction indicates how far the Net has to go in driving that process. What closes the gap? Brandwidth and the old-fashioned brand principles that underpin it: presence, relevance, differentiation, credibility, and imagery (user, usage, product, and associative).

HOW TO BUILD BRANDWIDTH

Building brandwidth means building a brand that

- ☐ explains the product or service;
- ☐ connects consumers' wants and needs;
- ☐ enhances the value of the product or service and the company from which it comes;
- ☐ distinguishes itself from all competitors and from the consumer sin of not doing anything at all.

The end result of building brandwidth is closing the sale. This isn't Haight-Asbury in the 1960s; this is the free market of the 2000s. You don't just want to be loved, you want to be paid.

Candidates running for president can't keep changing their tune—their basic issues—but they must keep adding to that tune, making it deeper and richer for more and more people. That's the political version of building brandwidth. And for the candidate, closing the sale means delivering the voter to the voting booth and getting him or her to pull the right lever.

But like all of the principles of e-marketing, building brandwidth isn't some new form of e-magic. It's all business; it's structure and process designed solely to deliver results. The world may be in a totally new age, but strong brands are built in the same way they have been forever. Markets are markets, as markets have been since the FedEx guy rode a camel. It's like architecture: No matter how the profession advances and what new shape Frank Gehry or I. M. Pei invents for his next museum or office building, the structure will still be built with a solid foundation and strong superstructure in accord with the laws of physics. Violate those laws, and you have a building that collapses in a cloud of dust.

Brands today and tomorrow will be built the way they were yesterday: They will be built on the basics. In our work creating brand strategies for everything from sneakers to software to soda pop to securities, we've seen the same rules apply again and again to the development, growth, and management of brands. It's the same on the Net as it is for the BAMs (bricks and mortars). Strong brands are developed along five key dimensions:

Presence
Relevance
Differentiation
Credibility
Imagery—user, usage, product, and associative

A strong brand strategy includes a plan for each one.

Presence

Presence in the marketplace is the way any brand gains consumers' awareness and acceptance. For packaged goods, market presence is usually achieved through distribution. Seeing the product on the shelf, consumers reason, "If it's widely distributed, it must be okay."

Brands extend their presence with advertising, merchandising, promotions, PR, and sponsorships. These create basic brand awareness and should also help drive other brand attributes, because it's quite clear that awareness does not necessarily translate into pur-chase intent or purchase. On the Net, distribution used to be all that was necessary to achieve awareness and trial among early adopters. It was, in the sense of packaged goods, a small supermarket with only a few shelves. Now, of course, those shelves extend for miles and miles, carrying almost a hundred million Web pages. It's very easy now for an e-brand to get lost. Internet brands have tried to increase their presence by linking to other sites or advertising on other sites. In addition, as we've said, many e-brands are now using mainstream media to build awareness and drive traffic to their site.

Considering the advantage that packaged goods or BAM retail brands have with their signage, merchandising, and packaging con-stantly in consumers' faces, often in their very own pantry, it's amaz-ing how successfully some Web brands have established at least awareness. 123Greetings.com, for instance, has roughly twice the number of unique visitors that the venerable Hallmark has. Why? How about the "Cup a Soup" name? What's a card all about, any-way? Some seemingly tiny Net players, like RedHat.com, MP3.com, and BlueMountain.com, have awareness equal to that of brands like Netscape or Intel among Internet users.

Of course, there's another component of market presence at work on the Net: viral marketing. Although consumer testimony is impor-tant in every product or service category, it's unusually important among Internet users, who supplement their personal and phone conversations with e-mail chat, the Net's answer to the water cooler. Word of mouth is the most compelling medium of advertising there is. **Consumer talk creates what we call "activated presence."** Prod-uct on shelves, Web site, merchandising and promotion at point of sale, wide distribution, posters on a fleet of delivery trucks, radio or TV—all of the brand presence possible—can become invisible if the brand's presence is not activated in the marketplace through word of mouth or, what is often more important, visible usage.

In the beer business, for example, the bar is the incubator of new brand choices. Those choices are driven not by advertising, but by beer drinkers leading other beer drinkers to new ideas in the market.

In America, most sales managers for any kind of product realize a truism that defines at once the simplicity and the complexity of the marketing process: "Selling stuff is what sells stuff." **Create usage in the marketplace: This creates more usage. It's visible sales and usage of your product in the marketplace that motivate others to try it.** A momentum will build that will drive the herd of users.

Obviously, telling you that you need sales in order to get sales is a little like telling a first-time job applicant, "You need experience for this job."

"But how do I get experience, if you won't hire me?"

How do you get usage in order to build usage? The answer is any way you can. It's a fact of basic marketing that you buy your first sale and often several more after that with promotion: price promotion coupons, free sampling, contests, and the like. The strongest communication of brand, bar none, is the product experience—the way the energy bar tastes, the way the car test-drives, the way the Web site does what you hoped it would do. So repeat usage builds brandwidth like nothing else. The favorite promotional tactic on the Internet is captured in one four-letter word: FREE! In fact, this almost doesn't count as promotion: FREE is what people assume when they click onto virtually any site, like walking into virtually any store. And use of the service is most often free:

☐ At AutoByTel.com or AutoTrader.com, you search for the perfect used car, locating the exact model, year, color, options, and price you want at a dealer nearest to you, and you do it for free.
☐ At Deja.com, you learn about any kind of product for free, get expert advice, get the reactions of peers who have experience with the product, check the ratings on a number of dimensions of the product made by people like you, then click through to

purchase the product (on another free service) at the lowest available price.

☐ Getting stock quotes is free on TheStreet.com (though you pay if you want your quotes in real time, not delayed).

☐ You can get free Web access, free e-mail, and even a free computer (freecomputer.com). "Free" is a pretty compelling offer. But is it relevant? That's the relevant question.

All of these sites depend on sources of revenue other than direct payment by consumers for using the service. They get indirect payment for their services, such as revenues from companies who advertise on the site or co-marketing fees for links or click-throughs from companies who want to be connected to the site's franchise of users. e-Tailers from Amazon.com (books) to Fogdog.com (sporting goods) to the e-commerce pages on sites like StarWars.com charge margins traditionally, but certainly not traditional margins. They pass along their enormous savings on BAM infrastructure. And although their infrastructure costs are a fraction of those of traditional retailers (for example, even with the warehouse system they're building, Amazon's overhead is still miniscule relative to a traditional retailer like Barnes & Noble), their marketing communications costs will be much, much higher in order to build awareness equal to that of BAM market presence (visibility of the store in the malls, etc.). The tactics of price promotion and free trial are timeless. They work . . . for a while. But building brandwidth works better over the long haul. And won't haul you into bankruptcy court. **Convincing consumers it's worth paying a premium for your product is the best business model there is.**

Many sites, though providing free service, ask consumers to register and provide information about themselves—name, e-mail address, and more, if they can get it. In the Internet economy, captured customer information is considered a valuable asset, almost as valuable as actual captured customers. Portals obviously have the best chance of capturing customer information, since they operate on a subscription basis, but the next best thing is to become a "virtual portal," the site Web consumers go to first and where they spend the most time. The ideal is to become their "gate-keeper," a trusted source of information, advice, advertising, and links. In return for a consumer's registration information, e-commerce sites will customize their site to his or her needs and wants. And that's a very powerful branding device. It builds return business more successfully than anything else. Jeff Bezos of Amazon.com has said, "We're willing to redecorate the store for every single user, every time they come in."

The more personal the experience, the more likely the consumer is to come back to it—and remember our definition of the purpose of ANY marketing activity: to convince more people to come back more often to buy more and be willing to pay more (though the "be willing to pay more" part is barely being tested on the Net). The business-to-business marketplaces, like those from our client, Commerx (CommerxPlastics and CommerxPackaging), Chemdex and Metalsite, require registration in order to use the exchange. Buyers register to extend their opportunity to find source materials such as plastic resins, machinery, and everything else they buy, from industrial cleaners to stationery and staples. This extension of opportunity allows them to access the highest quality and lowest prices: well worth registering with the best service. The same extension of opportunity is opened up for sellers—huge new territories that don't require huge new sales forces. It's a win-win for buyers and sellers and a win for the marketplace that captures the lion's share of them in any industrial ecosystem. Such marketplaces will derive a small commission on transactions and, to increase revenue, increasingly are offering additional higher-premium solutions and consulting services to their buyers and sellers.

FREE! has certainly been "seen" on the Net as a promotional offer; it's not an attraction per se, but table stakes for playing on the

Net. Indeed, in the B2C (business-to-consumer) space, this is the established value system: All the good stuff is free. A new portal by the name of IWin.com has been developed by Mark and Eric Stroman, two brilliant young men who gained recognition developing promotions in the entertainment business ("Win Bart Simpson's House!") and are the closest thing the Internet has to P. T. Barnum. IWin.com is trying to raise those table stakes. Use of the site not only is free, but enters the user into daily, weekly, and quarterly sweepstakes that give away millions of dollars in cash prizes. Like all marketing insurgents, they will at first be dismissed by the incumbent portals as insignificant ballyhoo. But we won't be surprised if we see YippeeIwonmoney. com or DoyoureallywanttobeanAOLmillionaire.com in the very near future. Net consumers are curious, and their experience on the Internet convinces them that there's always a new choice just a click or two away. IWin.com will get trial, and if it provides good service and support to its users, the big guys are going to have to "see" its sweepstakes format. Just how much you're willing to give away, and for how long, is a considerable issue. To make marketing work, you have to convince consumers to be willing to give a little back after a while—and be willing to pay more. We can't say it often enough.

To be successful, any brand in any category must develop activated presence through its market users and usage. Few brands can afford to develop presence using the carpet-bombing approach: mass distribution and mass advertising. What's important is to develop and activate presence among selected targets by essentially surrounding them with the brand. In e-marketing, as in all marketing, it's important to pick your shots.

Politicians adhere to a key principle that can help you develop market presence effectively and efficiently. It's "do the doable." What it means is don't break your pick on objectives that can't be achieved. Segment the users you want to move and CAN move. Don't ask people for a donation or a vote unless you have a fair chance of getting it. It isn't worth the time and effort. To help pick their shots, politicians segment their markets by attitude, not just by demographics. After all, attitude tells a lot more than race, age, or income does about how likely somebody is to vote. This is what the attitude spectrum looks like:

HO SO UNDECIDED SOS HAS

HO The Hard Opposition. They'll come out and vote against you in a blinding snowstorm. They hate you and the horse you rode in on, so you don't want to waste a kilowatt of energy trying to win them over. You write them off. The marketing equivalent is the competition's brand loyalist. Ungettable.

SO The Soft Opposition. They favor the opposition, but a light drizzle would dissuade them from going out to vote for them. Your job is to avoid enflaming this segment with issues that would move them: Don't give them a reason to vote. You want them to stay home on election day. In marketing, the soft opposition are mostly loyal to another brand. But with the endless election day of the marketplace, you may be able to win some of them over to your brand over time. Indeed, a lot of these consumers are brand-oriented buyers—the only problem is they've picked the wrong brand.

UNDECIDED If you were running for office, you'd do anything legal to win these votes. After all, you need only that 50.1% on Election Day. You'd seek out their influencers and try to win their support. You'd drive them to the polls. You'd run negative ads to try to influence their vote the night before the election. If you alienate them in the process, you've got two or four or six years to win them back, right?

In marketing, though, moving the undecided gets very expensive. There's an election every day in your market—sometimes hundreds of them. Are you ready to be buying their votes over and over again?

And remember the immortal words of a former Tammany Hall ward heeler: "The problem is, you buy those votes and they don't STAY bought."

Granted, you're going to buy the first sale . . . maybe several more. Marketing doesn't get efficient until there is repeat purchase, VOLUNTARY repeat purchase. e-Marketing doesn't get efficient until you've got loyal usage. If you have to essentially keep paying people to use your product, then it's not very valuable to them. Push marketing depends on distribution and promotion to make it easier to buy the product than not to buy it, but pull marketing is where the money is; this is when consumers are attracted to your product and pull the purchase themselves. On the Net, you can use any number of promotional tricks. IWin.com won't be the last one the Stromans come up with, and it won't be the last "raise you" in the portal wars. But eventually you have to prove value, to get people to use your service voluntarily, because it works for them, answering their needs and desires.

 SOS The Soft Support. These voters prefer you, but they may not vote. Your job is to give them more and more reasons to come out and vote for you, moving them from soft support to hard support. In e-marketing, this means building brandwidth, layer after layer of reasons to purchase and continue to purchase your brand, to come back more often to buy more. On the Internet there are plenty of visitors. There's plenty of window-shopping, but not enough sticking around and not enough purchasing. So the task is the same as in politics, giving them more reasons to vote for you, piling on the reasons until they do. This is what building brandwidth is all about. The goal in e-marketing and all marketing is to move these occasional users to heavier usage, toward brand loyalty.

The movement of current brand users toward greater brand use is what Bill Gates calls "the annuity stream." These folks are in your brand franchise, but they're on the outskirts, not close to the core of loyalty. They like the brand, they visit your site, but they don't register, they don't buy. They're tough to close. Still, they're there for the marketing toward greater support, and it's been estimated that it's six times cheaper to get increased sales out of current customers than to develop new users from the uninitiated. Microsoft focuses most of its marketing resources on what they call the "installed base," people who use Windows or one of their applications, such as Word or PowerPoint. Microsoft marketing and sales try to build brandwidth in "depth and breadth." "Depth" means selling people every upgrade of the software they already own. "Breadth" means selling them more Microsoft products along the product line—cross-selling, in other words. Get that many people to buy just one more Microsoft product, and it becomes the most valuable company in the galaxy.

Get these people in the franchise and do whatever it takes to hold them. Pure marketing efficiency means brand loyalty, customers who will use your product or service 100% of the time and even increase their usage. You'll hear us say it again and again: Usage builds loyalty. Make people like the brand, and then they'll use the product? That's a long shot. The sure shot in marketing is that usage leads to brand loyalty. That's why "branding usage" is so important. To use Microsoft as an example again, just a few years ago the company found through research that almost a third of Windows users didn't realize the product came from Microsoft (Attorney General Janet Reno clearly wasn't one of them). Although people were using Windows, they weren't seeing the Microsoft brand. The company quickly moved to rectify the situation.

One of our clients, eTour.com, struggled with the fact that surfing was perceived by the broad stripe of Net users as kind of uncool. Rather than try to scale that wall of skepticism, Jim Lanzone and Roger Burnette of eTour took our advice to focus on the hard support: dedicated Net surfers. They decided to own surfing as a category. And they've pretty much succeeded with their positioning, "surfing without searching." Next they'll move to focus on occasional surfers. Year 4 of the marketing plan calls for moving toward nonsurfers. By then, eTour will have the brandwidth to attract and hold these nonusers.

You should fight against "virtual consumption," whereby people prefer your brand but are quite willing to consume another; they don't perceive or care about the difference. And you should fight "unconscious consumption," whereby people use your product without knowing they're using it; often it's just a habit. People should be aware of the brand as they purchase it and as they consume it. The branding should help remind them of what's different and better about your product or service. You've got to make your differences make a difference and you've got to connect those differences to your brand if people are to associate it with your brand and want to come back more often to buy more. That's moving the soft support to hard support.

HAS   The Hard Support. These are your loyalists. You must keep their vote, their dollar, at all costs. Nothing in the world develops brandwidth like this core of walking, talking loyal users. Nobody's ever come up with better advertising than the testimony and visible consumption of your loyal users. Even usage of commodity products should be branded. People told the CEO of Starbucks he'd never get more than a quarter for a cup of java. But he believed in the power of a high-quality product and a high-quality brand. Maybe more importantly, he believed the brand could envelop the experience of the product. The next time you're in a Starbucks laying down $4.50 for a cup of coffee, take a look around the store and see how thoroughly and thoughtfully they've branded the environment. It's unmistakably Starbucks, even when you carry it out. You should try to do that good a job of branding usage, particularly among your loyalists. Turn them into walking, talking billboards— in other words, brand your users, too. When your brand carries a certain amount of social currency, your users are happy to wear it as a badge. This has always been Budweiser's advantage. It certainly works for Nike and Tommy Hilfiger and Polo and Gap. T-shirts and coffee cups and now the omnipresent fleece pullover are always a part of a new brand launch on the Net. It seems like simplistic branding, but the fact is, the stuff works. And on the Net, you're looking for any way you can to extend brand presence. These are the remarkable unpaid endorsers of your brand—you've got to love them.

@   @   @

The Internet allows highly active management of the customer relationship, moving along this path from soft to hard support, developing the relationships and building brandwidth through a constant, intuitive interaction, constantly customizing and personalizing the service, transferring ownership to the consumer. Free e-mail, anyone? Want a customized foyer for your Net portal? e-Marketers do a lot for these key people. But you really can't do enough. Think about lifetime value. Think about that "annuity stream."

So think about your customer segments in terms of attitude. And think about the rewards relative to required effort of focusing on the soft support. The movement of soft support to hard support in any market creates that sense of brand vitality and activity that leads to brand momentum. Remember, it takes sales to build sales; it takes usage to build usage. Turning occasional brand users into loyalists means turning on that vital and highly efficient means of advertising.

In fact, we've found it's useful to think of any communication targets in terms of attitude. If you're a manager, think of the people who report to you in terms of attitude. How many are undecided about your leadership? How many are soft supporters? Hard supporters? We've found that the squeaky wheels in any organization are usually among the soft opposition. But what Spiro Agnew infamously referred to as the "silent majority" is among the soft support. Your time and effort will often get pulled to the squeaky wheels and away from the quiet supporters. But real progress in any group will be made by spending time and effort to engage and activate the soft support. **This is where the primary focus of e-marketing must be. You must be developing ways to move your current users to more and more productive usage.**

Developing market presence is just the first part of this long process.

Relevance

Brand relevance is the way your brand fits into your customers' lives and how it meets their needs and desires. It's how important your brand becomes to your customers. So it's about personalization—the more it addresses the needs and wants of its users, the more brandwidth it will develop. Most Net marketers realize this. In Net terms, personalization is "sticky." That's why you see My Yahoo!, My eToul, etc., allowing you—indeed, begging you—to design your own start page and a more personalized service. This personalized Net marketing is another sign of the end of mass marketing and the end of optimization in manufacture. **On the Net, customization rules. Internet companies accept a key principle ignored by many other marketers: Fixate on the customer, not on the product or the competition.** The customer interface is direct—you're literally connected to the customer at all times. We learned this principle in politics but proved its veracity in our corporate work, as well: Democracy is dialogue, and dialogue is critical to building brandwidth. More democracy is better. Fluid democracy, an ongoing interactive conversation with your customers, is the best thing of all. The Net allows this conversation to flow 24-7. In that conversation, you learn what's important to them. You learn relevance on their terms, the most personal terms. This allows you to develop your customer benefit or unique selling proposition on their terms. Again and again, we see Internet marketers boasting in marketing communications about what their technology does. They forget to bridge the relevance on the customers' terms: "What does it do for me??"

Another Z Group client, Buymedia.com, offers a simple but highly relevant advantage to its advertiser clients: proprietary systems that speed analytical information about the media buy. Find out what people really care about and find a way to deliver it—better yet, deliver it in a proprietary way. The old media buying market was a "black box" model: "We're the only ones who understand how this is really done." Like the Wizard says in *The Wizard of Oz*, "Ignore that man behind the curtain." The essence of the new model is to make the process transparent and easy for marketers to operate.

Tech companies often get caught up in communicating attributes and fail to translate the attributes into real benefit for consumers. To understand that real benefit to your customers, you've got to be in a conversation with them. Direct is best, but sensitive market research is the next best thing.

- □ Learn relevance on the most personal terms.
- □ Learn about opportunities to sell them more stuff more often. Why and when would your customers like more?
- □ Learn about the competitive set from your customers' perspective. Who do THEY think is a good alternative to you?
- □ Learn what's keeping your customers from greater brand commitment. They're quite willing to tell you what would help you to build more brandwidth with them. You can decide if you can afford to meet their terms and still make money. In this

way, all of e-marketing is a reverse auction; in dialogue with customers, they will tell you what they want and need, and you can bid to meet the wants and needs profitably.

There's no such thing as developing TOO MUCH relevance. Just keep building brandwidth, layering on the meaning, piling on ways to prove you understand your customers' needs, desires, and personal quirks better than anybody else. The *Wall Street Journal Interactive*, for example, has done a fabulous job of building brandwidth by building benefits on benefits. If you're a subscriber, you constantly receive relevant e-mails advising you of yet another service they're offering that will make your life easier and better.

It's like the mating ritual: Just keep becoming more and more a part of their lives. To do that, do research to learn more about your customers' lives. And, please, not qualitative research. There's no problem with qualitative research companies—the problem is with qualitative research group members. For their $50 fee, they go to the session and feel like it's their job to tell you what you want to hear. Not so in quantitative research. So do that, and do lots of it.

Differentiation

If you want to create a positive return on investment, there's one sure way to do it: Own the position of relevant differentiation in your marketplace. You've got to have meaning in your customers' lives, and you've got to be perceived as different from all competitors. Differentiation is where value is created on the Net or anywhere else.

Value is developed by the scarcity of something that people want or need. OPEC gets this pretty well, don't you think? When oil prices go down, they limit production to make it more scarce, more valuable. Value is created by scarcity. There's no value in sameness.

So why is it that the most frequently used market position is essentially, "me, too!" The market leader makes a claim, and the market followers quickly say, "Me, too!" The followers think it's necessary to "see" the leader.

"Whiter whites," says the leader.

"Me, too!" echo all the followers.

"Cheaper books online," says the leader.

"Me, too!" echo the followers.

It may be necessary to "see" the leader. But forming up around the leader's definition of strategic differentiation in the marketplace really only reinforces their lead. When the rest of the market says, "We agree. Whiter whites are important," there's no reason for consumers to leave the market leader.

It's differentiation—"raise you," not "see you"—that creates defection from the incumbent. It's differentiation that encourages trial of a new concept. **It's differentiation that changes the market dialogue and takes it away from the leader.** "Be different, or be damned," said the late, great Roberto Goizueta of Coca-Cola.

So you must design differences into your product and your marketing. Relevant difference must be driven into every aspect of marketing communications, from distribution, to positioning, to advertising, to promotion, to events and sponsorships, and on and on. You must design difference into every aspect of your customer relationship. Differentiation is in the details, and it's in the tiniest details that it's proved. **Remember, it's your best customers— those who visit you most often—who will notice the details most surely.** They will help communicate them to others.

This is what ComputerJobs.com has done to distinguish itself from the 80 or so other job boards on the Net. The details all communicate that this is a place for career management and guidance, not just getting your next job. "Upgrade your future, not just your job" is their positioning, and it resonates with both job applicants and their corporate clients. But with 80 competitors on the Internet,

ComputerJobs.com still won't get much chance to relax and enjoy their advantages. They'll have to continually search out new opportunities to differentiate themselves positively.

Whether you market on or off the Net, streamline your marketing communications around the issues that will make a difference. Don't clutter your own messages with irrelevant or undifferentiated babble. Take a look at the products in any marketplace, from soapsuds to SUVs. Why is it that almost all of them list the same two or three top attributes? Even the most different products in the category pull themselves back into the pack with this repetition of what they guess are the requisite table stakes in that market. Ridiculous! Keep to the stuff that builds value and brandwidth: relevant differentiation. Lose the rest. Funnel your customers' attention and interest toward the things that will make it clear you are providing unique benefits to them.

When you feel you have a market advantage, make sure you communicate it loudly and clearly. Abandon subtlety, as CNET.com has learned to do after spending multimillions on the subtle and strange approach. Obscuring the point is a remarkably common approach among Net advertisers. Your ad agency is likely to scold you for being "too obvious" if you ask whether it would be okay to mention your brand in the new commercial. Like the penchant for weird naming that used to exist on the Internet, there seems to be an accepted premise that users will appreciate subtlety in advertising more than clarity. But it's the simple ideas that have succeeded: Amazon.com, Priceline.com, e-Trade.com, and so on. As competitive clutter increases, the need for clarity increases. **If your product is "me, too!" and you're trying to establish differentiation in your advertising, you're in big trouble. You're focusing on the wrong problem.** It's one thing to get crowded out of recognition by the competition, but it's inexcusable to get lost because your relevant differentiation is disguised behind advertising that's artful to the point of obscurity.

Credibility

Every brand is a promise. It carries with it a set of expectations defined by users' experience and by your marketing claims. Brand credibility is increased by delivering on that promise. Research for Microsoft during the late 1980s showed low levels of customer satisfaction, and it was vexing to Microsoft to see the low scores customers gave their applications software. These customers' reactions were probed in qualitative research: "Why do you feel so bad about Microsoft's products?"

They had no problem with the products, it turned out. They'd shrug and say, "I don't know how I'm SUPPOSED to feel. All they do in the advertising is talk about the attributes of the software . . . about performance stuff. But what's it supposed to do for ME? What's the benefit?"

This shows how important it is to always bridge to personal relevance, to customer benefit, to "what's in it for ME?" **It also shows you can't deliver on customer satisfaction unless you clearly define the customer benefit in advance. We developed a simple reminder: D & D. Define expectations, and deliver on them.** As we continued to look at the important issue of customer satisfaction over the years, we refined our thinking. Today, we use the model of Southwest Airlines:

Year in and year out in the airline industry, Southwest Airlines is the number 1 brand for customer satisfaction. Southwest doesn't deliver first-class seating, or even assigned seating. They don't deliver gourmet meals or fine wines. What they DO deliver is their promises—inexpensive, frequent flights between business destinations. No frills, no BS. Southwest overdelivers on service attitude. Their recruiting objective is attitude first, aptitude second. One reason they can be so friendly and helpful is that their service personnel aren't engaged in arguments about seat assignments or missed upgrades at the boarding gate. You get what you get on a first-come, first-served basis.

Now, consider their competition: American, United, Northwest, or Delta. Since Z Group is headquartered in Atlanta, Georgia, Delta's hub, where they control about 80% of the flights on any given day, we are hostages of the airline. You've seen their commercials. This is how they define expectations in advance: You see a handsome guy sitting in first class. His tie is loosened. He's totally relaxed. The seat next to him is empty. It's serene and quiet. A beautiful flight attendant is handing him a glass of fine wine. When was the last time your airline delivered on those kind of promises? Personally, we're 0 for 3 million miles on that kind of service. Because they have defined expectations so unrealistically, Delta, United, and the other airlines cannot possibly deliver, much less overdeliver. And claiming what they can't deliver only rubs it in. As frequent flyers, we're rankled when we hear the captain of the hub airline come on the intercom as we're rolling up to the gate: "We realize you have a choice when you fly and we're just sure glad you chose us."

What's the choice? Greyhound?

Unless it's been legislated for you, your company probably doesn't have the stranglehold on your market that the airlines have on theirs. **And if you don't increase your brand's credibility with customers' every use of your product and with your every interaction with customers, you're going to lose them. Credibility is living up to your promises. Don't make ones you can't keep.**

We're involved with Netcentives. They realized early on that Net B2C categories would be awash in sameness and so value gets commoditized. And "differentiated value" is the battle cry of Netcentives. It started with a system of "frequent flyer points" on the Web for purchases, but it has evolved into a system that helps e-companies do whatever it takes to add value in their marketplace. To do so, Netcentives continues to acquire and invent companies to keep differentiating their own business model. That's why they're successful.

Imagery

Brand imagery is easy to picture for a brand like Coca-Cola, with its red disk, the polar bears, Santa, or the distinctive Spencerian script of the logo. McDonald's has the golden arches and the "Mc" naming architecture. Nike has the swoosh and had Michael Jordan. Microsoft has Bill Gates, the Michael Jordan of the information revolution. **The fact is, all brands have imagery associated with them, some of it good and some of it lousy. Good brands have shaped that imagery into meaning and differentiation.** Yahoo! does this. e-Trade does it, too. Think of the way Gateway has used its cowhide imagery in secondary packaging.

We divide imagery into four categories: user imagery, usage imagery, product imagery and associative imagery. To be successful in building brandwidth, you have to be successful in building every one of these kinds of imagery.

The fact is, ALL products have these four kinds of imagery in them, waiting to be tapped. But very, very few of them turn the tap.

User imagery is about what kind of people use your product. The ideal—people like me, people I like, people I'd like to be like. Soft drink ads, with their young, hip, good-looking people, are an obvious example. If the advertising is for Depends undergarments, expect June Allison to represent the user, not the manufacturer.

Usage imagery is about what it feels like to use your product and be associated with your brand. In e-marketing, the usage imagery you want is SMART, as in, "I feel really smart for using Priceline.com."

Product imagery is the direct image of the product and the product in use. Think iMac: Steven Jobs, who's always being sold short as a techie and long as a marketer, also happens to be an incredibly good intuitive designer. Think VW Beetle.

Associative imagery is about the company you keep—the brands, individuals, institutions, and events closely identified with your brand. Buick and PGA golf. Amazon.com and Sotheby's. Disney, McDonald's, and Coke. Microsoft and NBC.

Your brand is a disk filled with the 1s and 0s of every impression your customers have of your company and products or services: every communication, every interaction, the usage of your product or service, the impressions of other users—every detail. **Your brand is defined in your customers' perceptions. It's their party, and their perceptions form our reality as marketers. So you must understand and constantly show that you respect their perspective and attitudes.** You must constantly be building the brand relationship along the dimensions of presence, relevance, differentiation, credibility, and imagery, just as you must continue to develop any personal relationship, or see it fade. And just like an interpersonal relationship, to make it last, you have to keep it fresh and new. You must shape the meaning of the tiniest details of communications, because they make a difference, they define the brand. And you can't be sure which one is most important to which customer at any given moment. Nothing is NOT important in building brandwidth. Your brand, after all, will be the most valuable asset you ever build in your company. Nothing else will come close.

DESIGNING BRAND ARCHITECTURE

You reinforce the strength of your company brand or top product brand by developing a coherent and strong brand architecture around it. It's like building a moat around your differentiation. Brand architecture is the link, the clear relationship, between one brand and another within your brand portfolio (Coke, Diet Coke, Cherry Coke, for instance).

At Broadband Sports their main product is AthletesDirect, which links fans to the websites of hundreds of athletes. Fans have found that some athletes prefer to break personal news in their own words on their own Web sites rather than see them interpreted by sportswriters. Broadband's founder, Tyler Goldman, had acquired a number of other Web services targeted to the almost insatiable hunger for detail that the most avid sports fans have: RotoNews (for fantasy league players) and CSX and PSX (in-depth college and pro sports coverage by top sportswriters). In an increasingly crowded sports market on the Net, this smallish company needed to define itself and its territory clearly, or be confused with and probably squashed by the big league players, like ESPN.com, FoxSports.com and CBS's Sportsline.com. So Broadband linked its acquisitions and new developments together and positioned themselves around the best known of their services, AthletesDirect, creating AthletesDirect, RotoNewsDirect, TeamsDirect, SportwritersDirect. And they linked them all to the corporate parent with this common positioning: "Direct to the Hard-Core Sports Fan."

With brand architecture, you create the dots your customers will connect to form the total picture of your company's meaning. Each product or service in your portfolio helps define and strengthen the next one. As we've mentioned before, the paragon of brand architecture is McDonald's. They use the "Mc" convention in almost all of their new product naming. And they use the golden arches as the "M" in McDonald's to reinforce the visual differentiator. One of the most effective brand communications anywhere is the little red and gold "M" symbol with an arrow on highways all over the country. Here's a company with close to a 100% brand recognition. "They don't even need brand architecture," you may say.

If not, it's because they've built it up so successfully. And they'll keep on building it. Link your company brands with language and visual imagery. **Define a clear outline around the things that commonly differentiate your company's products in the marketplace. This is just another way of defining your market differentiation.**

e-Lessons:

☐ The Internet is as crowded a brand environment as exists today. You must define your brand carefully and communicate its definition clearly and repetitively. You must build brandwidth: Build your brand's market presence and make sure to activate its presence; develop relevant meaning and differentiation relative to your competitive set; increase your brand's credibility by defining and relentlessly expanding its imagery.

☐ You must develop a coherent brand architecture within your company that links the corporate trademark, product brands, sub-brands, and branded product benefits in a familylike structure.

☐ Remember that brands on the Internet need constant refreshment and revitalization. While staying true to core meaning, keep expanding the meaning of your brand in personal terms, constantly adding value and occasionally some surprises. One aspect of traditional branding that's obsolete in this new age of e-marketing is the steadfast unchangeability of brands. In this highly interactive age, authenticity can now be established quickly. Customers can get to know you very well very quickly.

The brand relationship needs a little juicing up on occasion, just like a marriage. The brand that stands still today is dead tomorrow. There is no such thing as the status quo in branding.

□ If you're not building brandwidth, the forces of the market will be unbuilding it for you.

5

WHAT'S RELEVANT IS COOL—
BUT WHAT'S COOL ISN'T
ALWAYS RELEVANT

Both of us had the opportunity to work in the advertising business (back in the days when the earth was cooling), so we can be seen as naturally sympathetic to the industry. But we both have the scars to prove that we tried unsuccessfully over the years to change the fundamental architecture of the advertising business. We keep hoping another David Ogilvy will come along and start changing the way the business is approached (and maybe that next "David" will be Shelly Lazarus, the brilliant chair of WPP Group's Ogilvy Communications).

We've been loud and clear in saying what we have to say about the state of advertising on and about the Web today. And our criticism hasn't been focused on the ad agencies alone. As the great Ogilvy observed about bad advertising, "Every client gets the advertising they deserve."

Advertising is a key component of the total marketing mix. It consumes billions of dollars and generates many billions more in the U.S. economy and around the world. Advertising works—or some of it does—but most of it doesn't work as hard as it should. Far too much of it is lazy in focus and effort.

To criticisms of advertising its defendants respond, "Yes, but judging advertising is so subjective."

No, it's not. **When advertising works, it sells. That's not subjective.** It sells the product, the concept, or the company. It closes the sale. It sells current customers on increased usage and new customers on trial. It builds brandwidth. When advertising doesn't sell, it's not working.

"But it's building awareness, even though it's not creating sales."

Oh, come on! Awareness is a long way from the sale in the process of awareness, consideration, trial, purchase, reconsideration, retrial, repurchase. And, remember, profitability doesn't really kick in until "repurchase." It's possible to be aware of a brand and not buy it. In the next 30 seconds, you can probably list ten or twenty brands you know well but have never used. Have you ever used Kotex? If you have, have you ever used Gillette Foamy Shave Cream?

Awareness isn't enough. Advertising must sell. It must differentiate from the pack of competitors and connect to an audience of one, and another, and another, and another . . . It must add velocity to the sponsor company's business objectives.

"But our advertising is supposed to build brands and bond people to them, not build sales."

And what the hell are brands supposed to do if not help sell stuff? Why do we have them in the first place? To get consumers to bond with the brand?

Bond with this: Advertising is supposed to sell, SELL, **SELL!**

After taking a pretty healthy swipe at the ad business in *The End of Marketing As We Know It,* why devote an entire chapter in this new book to advertising? After all, companies and agencies are now rethinking and retooling their relationships. Not a week goes by without Procter & Gamble or another giant announcing yet another new way of judging the performance or computing the compensation of their agencies. Agencies are under tremendous pressure to become a more serious partner in reaching a client's sales and marketing goals. Under the thumb of unhappy clients, the agencies are hiring consultants of their own and executives from nontraditional agency backgrounds to help change the dialogue in the industry.

So things are looking up, right? Wrong. *The End of Marketing As We Know It* was published before the beginning of e-marketing as we've come to know it. And e-marketing has taken advertising to new heights—of stupidity. As we work with startup Internet companies at Z Group, we find that things are worse in the world of advertising than we thought they were even a year or two ago.

Creativity defined as finding creative ways to communicate a highly relevant and differentiated sales message is on the decline. Creativity defined as finding obscure ways to tell jokes on network television at a cost of hundreds of thousands of dollars a minute is on the rise.

Why? Advertising spending goes up, up, up. Indeed, the dot.coms' move into offline advertising has revitalized their economics. These days, whenever we call an ad agency about handling the account of one of our new Web companies, we hear the same refrain: "Well, of course, we'd love to help you out. But we're just too, too busy right now."

In this economic boom, this Mother of All Booms, with every dynamic of our economy producing at record levels, why is advertising achieving less? Let's take a closer look.

WHAT'S HAPPENING IN THE DOT.COM WORLD?

Somewhere out there in a converted warehouse is a potential new advertising client, a spanking new Web startup. They don't know much about marketing. After all, the people who started this business are engineers, not marketers. They invented a dot.com that is based on technology, not marketing prowess. Their expertise is digital 1s and 0s, not headlines and body copy. They established themselves on a good measure of hope and the meager confidence and checkbooks of a few friends and family members. Here is where the art often overtakes substance. If the customer or consumer doesn't understand your message, it's wasted. Period. **For years marketing decision makers have been intimidated into believing that if a message is incomprehensible to them it may be cool enough for their market. Don't buy it. The rule of market messaging to any group is, keep it simple**.

The Web entrepreneurs are young and very new to business—in fact, they're very new to EVERYTHING. They work tirelessly toward their goals, sleeping on the office floor, using a couple of empty pizza boxes for a pillow. And one day, most often way too soon, they decide they want to do something that's a lot more refreshing than writing code and trying to convince potential investors that they're for real. They want to do some advertising. After the gruesome process of getting the startup jump-started, they want to start telling people all about their new ideas. They want to find an advertising agency and create some of that fun, irreverent advertising they've been seeing the last few years for one dot.com after another. They want a bunch of hip young people like them to create exciting words and graphics about their product. They want an ad on TV or a fun promotion or maybe to get their name in the *Wall Street Journal*.

For once, like Cyndi Lauper said about girls in the 1980s, they "just want to have fun."

So before a marketing strategy or even an advertising brief is written, VOILA—they have an ad agency, a promotion house, or a PR company on the line. They go to the agency's cool loft offices and feel the warmth of recognition. Do you want skim milk in that latte? People there are glib and charming. They are dressed to the nines in the latest tones of black on black. They sit you down in conference rooms and show entertaining commercials, cool press programs, and way-cool promotional T shirts and hats and trinkets and trash. "This is what we can do for you, too." The strategy?? Later. Right now . . . would you like another cappuccino? What's not to like? And they want you to like them so very, very much.

It's amazing to see how thoroughly ad agencies and PR and promotions companies embraced the Web. Most agencies were slow to catch onto the "Internet thing." The Net challenges the way they've made money for decades: network television and mass advertising. They treated it as another passing fancy—as a fashion event, not fundamental business evolution. So they create their own Internet specialists, sometimes spinning them off into little boutiques with cool-sounding names, also based on fashion, not business fundamentals. No suits. No serious faces. And the latest of everything, from office furniture to focaccia at lunch. It's like the Internet according to a Hollywood set designer: *Friends* meets the Net. They're a happy bunch in the agencies, and they're not faking it. This is as much fun as it looks.

Fun, yes. Serious business, no.

This is the state of marketing tactics in 2000. For the agency people, e-commerce and its pseudomarketing and advertising are a lot funner than the disciplined approach of most of today's blue chip marketers. No confining strategy; no cadre of brand managers to deal with. You want creative freedom? It's spelled d-o-t-c-o-m.

Most often, we get new clients AFTER they've run the big ad campaign. This was true of the Newspaper Association of America. The year before they hired us they'd run an ad campaign admonishing Americans to read newspapers, because "it's good for you." Take your medicine, dear. But this didn't confront the key issue the industry faces—the relevance of newspaper usage. This issue will have to be addressed on the ground, not over the airwaves. It's going to be done with the content and organization of the newspaper, with distribution and pricing, with merchandising, with ad sales and circulation and promotions and PR and advertising—with everything communicating.

This is the prevalent attitude in the ad industry about the Internet economy. It's fun and games. Of course, it's also wads and wads of money—THAT part, the agencies are taking very seriously, thank you.

Maybe you remember this advice from *The End of Marketing:* "You're not the target audience." But these agencies forget it immediately, and so do their clients. They assume the target audience is just the way they see themselves: cool, fashion-conscious, jokey and snide MTV viewers. If the ad guy wears a nose ring, he creates advertising with a nose ring. Big marketing clients would never have allowed the ad people to say and do the things they have routinely done and said in e-advertising. (The irony is that as we write this new book, the ad managers at those big marketing clients have decided they don't want to miss out on all this fun, so they're doing imitation Internet advertising for their products.)

The advertising is irreverent. It's intended just to be hip and fresh. It's supposed to make people love your brand. And the advertising storyboards they present to the startups are indeed irreverent and hip. It's interesting, we think, that every Internet idea seems to lend itself to broadcast TV advertising, according to the ad agencies. In one commercial storyboard we saw recently from a well-known creative agency, human feces was used as the attention-getter for one of our Z Group companies. Yeah, right. We've seen plenty of bad advertising before, but this takes the . . . um . . . cake. Fortunately, the e-managers who saw it had the same reaction we did.

We've seen literally everything presented to our clients—the rude and nude, the violent, the silly, and lots and lots of the stupid, and all of it blending together into a tasteless stew. You may remember the joke, but almost never the teller. The spot may get some awareness, but not consideration, much less purchase intent. It's just another joke out there in a swamp of bad jokes, in a sea of sameness. e-Business may not yet have many mature companies, but that's no reason for advertising, a business that's thrived in this country for 200 years, to be acting like a teenager.

Irreverent too often ends up irrelevant.

Why get so exercised about a few funny ads, some stupid press releases, and another coffee cup or fleece pullover with a Net company logo on it? What's the harm? Well, the harm isn't so much what these aimless tactics have done—though we'd love to have just 1% of the venture capital that has e-vaporated in the past two years in ineffective tactical campaigns—the harm is what these campaigns have FAILED to do.

Effective communications can build a business. Ineffective communications can hold one back. The PC revolution of the 1970s and 1980s was retarded in its growth and penetration of American business and culture because of what we called "the Revenge of the Nerds" effect. Most people in the PC hardware and software industry realized that ease of use would be the key issue in broadening the reach of the PC in work and at home. Bill Gates had mandated the mission of Microsoft as putting "a computer on every desk and in every home," which meant literally everybody everywhere would have to be using a computer. It would have to be as easy to use as a telephone or television. But there was an obstacle to this mission. It was the attitude of many of the product developers in the software and hardware companies, that "Revenge of the Nerds" effect. You could experience this attitude most directly if you called one of the PC 800-number support lines. "You mean, you don't know what RAM is?"

You take somebody who was in the Audiovisual Club in high school, pushed around by the jocks and Ivy Leaguers and rappers and almost everybody else. Now this guy's on the help end of a customer support line, with one of those idiots sitting in front of a frozen computer screen on the other end. REVENGE!

We saw some research on one software company's help line. They asked customers to make a wish list of what might improve service on their support line. Down that list at about number 16 was, "Solve my problem." All 15 of the answers above it had to do with the attitude of the support staff: "Just don't put me on hold for twenty minutes" . . . "Don't treat me like an idiot" . . . "Don't ask me if I'm sure I turned on the computer." Stuff like that. Consider the users' manual. Most people would rather reach into a bag of rattlesnakes than open up that book. The revenge attitude undoubtedly retarded the development of easier-to-use equipment, applications, and support materials.

That's why we worry about the "Animal House" effect in tactical marketing. In our work, we've tried to be tough on these suppliers for their own good and for ours, as marketing strategists, to get the essence of the brand communicated to achieve the results our clients need. The brilliance of a creative idea has often been the make-it-or-break-it last connection between the marketing strategy and the objectives it's trying to reach. And some of the top creative agencies in the country are our favorites to work with on or off the Net. Weldon and Weiden and Kennedy. Ogilvy. They just tend to be the smartest as well as the most creative. In our work, we've seen the best tactical marketing has to offer, and the best is not just about coming up with the funniest joke or winning the industry's biggest award. After all, in recent years many of the ad industry's most celebrated campaigns, such as the one with that strange smiling guy for

Nissan that was named campaign of the year by *Ad Age*, were eventually dropped for lack of results. In the evolution of business promised by the Internet economy, it's important that the support industries also evolve.

It's tough to beat a first-mover position with a product or service—either first in the category or the effective redefiner of an existing category.

Now, as never before, the e-conomy requires new ideas and different approaches. But what's new? Super Bowl advertising for techies? Apple's Steve Jobs and his fabulously talented creative director, Lee Clow of Chiat-Day (later swallowed by TBWA), made that move in 1984—16 Super Sundays ago—with what most people still consider the best television commercial of all time: A young athletic woman hurls a sledge-hammer through the blaring "Big Brother" on a huge video screen. Steve had to fight his own board of directors to get that ad on the air. But it was seminal in establishing Apple and the revolution of ease of use. Would it work today, 16 years later? Absolutely. In fact, Apple's new "Think Different" campaign is an extension of the "1984" position, done by its creators. The same is true of every great ad since Ivory soap symbolized its purity in the fact that it floats. Effective is timeless.

The Web is all about change, but it's about change based on the fundamentals. Amazon.com has changed the way many people buy books, but it's done so using the most fundamental and timeless approach of all the best merchants. Z Group works with Commerx, which has developed the evolved industrial marketplace, but its marketplaces are based on the essential principles that go back to the original market, the *Suk*, thousands of years ago. So we expect advertising to be based on fundamental marketing principles, and we expect change to be built on those fundamentals. With most of the Net advertising we see, there's no change and no fundamentals. Advertising should be leading this business evolution and the Internet revolution, by leading the definition of the future of the business. That would help open up opportunity wider and faster. It would help extend the opportunities of the Net to new users and new entrepreneurs. It would lend velocity to the information economy. Advertising—really good advertising that communicates relevance and differentiation clearly—will be more important than ever before in the new age of e-marketing.

In that new age, advertising with the nose ring will be long dead and buried.

CREATING E-ADVERTISING TO CLOSE THE SALE

So far, advertising created in the e-commerce space just hasn't taken the industry seriously. It's had its tongue in its cheek: "This is just a joke between us cool people, huh?" Advertising in e-marketing has taken the same cavalier attitude toward closing the sale that many CFOs have taken toward turning a profit. "Yeah, sure . . . someday." This advertising generally assaults convention and insults anybody who goes to work in a suit.

It brings to mind the supposed sequel to Apple's famous "1984" Super Bowl ad. After doing the best commercial in the history of advertising, Apple did one of the worst. The ad, called "Lemmings," ran during the 1985 Super Bowl. Research had been done after the 1984 ad that showed that thousands and thousands of PC users (at that time "PC" meant the IBM/Microsoft DOS-based personal computers, the dominant format) had been caught up in the Apple revolution, a lot of them motivated by that commercial. There was only one obstacle between those PC users and Apple: They simply felt they weren't really invited in.

Apple's previous advertising had developed user imagery that showed it to be the property of people who wore casual flannel shirts and jeans to work years before Casual Fridays. It was the property of people who worked in lofts, while most people were still in office buildings. It was the property of the young and restless. The rest of us, the poor jerks in business suits (remember, this was 1985) and serious shoes, just didn't feel we were welcome there, much as we wanted to be.

All Apple had to do was lower this obstacle and reach out and invite the PC users in. With this information in hand, the agency developed Apple's highly anticipated next act at the Super Bowl. "Lemmings" showed IBM types (according to the agency), businessmen and businesswomen wearing dark suits and carrying dark brief cases, walking off a cliff, somehow or other following IBM over the precipice. "Lemmings" slammed the door on those very people who wanted only to be invited in and all but stopped this market insurgent's incursion into the IBM franchise. At one point, Scott almost convinced Steve Jobs to run "Compliments of Apple Computer" on a white card during the Super Bowl, but was wrestled to the ground by the agency. Remarkably, it was the very same agency that only one year before had not only made history, but, maybe more rarely in the ad business, actually made something happen in the marketplace.

Think about the brilliance of Burger King's "flame-broiling versus frying" campaign against McDonald's. This had the people in Oak Brook running for cover. Fortunately for them, Burger King seems to lose its way every year or two and departs this solid marketing ground for something more creative and more ephemeral—and a lot less effective.

Internet Ads Most Often Trail the Market

Most of the advertising for Internet companies is aimed at the early adopter market, the techies who dominated Internet usage five years ago. So it's aiming behind the true nature of the market today.

It's like a duck hunter shooting behind the bird that's flying away: Most often, it's a miss. And in e-marketing, it's got to be all hits all the time. There's no time for the big miss. Not many companies will get the second or third or fourth try at the market that Apple has had. As we mentioned before, F. Scott Fitzgerald said, "In America, there are no second acts," and we think maybe he was predicting life on the Internet.

Advertising has to do what the product does—it has to perform. Below is a typical briefing we give an ad agency. It defines the job an ad must do. And it's a tough job.

The Ad Brief That We Give to the Agency

✓ *The ad has to create awareness for the brand, not just for the ad.*

✓ *The ad has to define the product. What's it for? If it's a new idea, what's it like?*

✓ *The ad has to define why the consumer should care about the product.*

✓ *The ad has to define the rational and emotional benefits of the product.*

✓ *The ad must help define the user, usage, product, and associative imagery of the product.*

Good tactical marketing programs are firing on all cylinders. The next time you see an ad or promotion or PR release, ask yourself, Is it doing all that? Is it doing ANY of that (beyond the awareness the company gets for pasting its name up in public)? Is it doing any of that in a way that's truly arresting and involving? If it is, give it your own personal award. It's very unusual these days.

The Chinese had it right more than two thousand years ago when they said, "Tell them and they will forget. Show them and they will remember. Involve them and they will understand."

Counting Eyeballs Doesn't Count

The Internet businesses we work with at Z Group and Core Strategy Group consider the Web VERY serious business. Yes, we see a lot of fresh, young faces. Plenty of Tevas. Their offices are often filled with toys and games. In fact, those offices look a little more like dormitories than offices. But they're dead serious about the business at hand. They have built their successes on a foundation of business fundamentals. These are ambitious people with a focus on wide success: They don't see the Net as the exclusive frat house of young people. They see it the way AOL sees itself—as an appliance that will be as ubiquitous as, but much more useful than, the telephone. They see this as the way business and communications will be conducted by most Americans in the very near future.

They envision Internet users as people who are mature and sensible—more mature and sensible than the current means of measuring success in Web marketing. Currently, the only measure is an eyeball count—determined by how many people click onto your site. But how many are just passing by? How many are learning important marketing information about your brand? How many are moving closer to purchase decisions? Those are the important measures.

Eyeball counting became the key Web measurement because the measuring companies assumed the Web was going to be a traditional advertising medium, like matchbook covers or magazine

pages. Early Web business plans assumed that advertising revenue would be a key element of profits. They predicted torrents of money. They got a trickle. The ratings agencies on the Net like to measure eyeballs because it's the easiest thing to measure—not because it's the most important measure of the effect of the site. Ad agencies love to measure reach and hate to be held accountable for sales. But reach is way short of results. Ad agencies also love to measure awareness, because even low awareness assumes they must be on the air or in the magazine—meaning they're getting paid to be judged, even if judged poorly. Bad awareness results just end up in more advertising and more commissions. But awareness isn't results; awareness doesn't even get you halfway there.

Measuring visits alone is a poor way to understand the power of Web marketing or the value of various Web businesses, because they are about interaction and involvement more than sight or sound. It's just like awareness is a poor measure of the effectiveness of e-marketing. That's why we looked at purchase intent in the study of Super Bowl ads, discussed in Chapter 1.

Indeed, our clients in the Newspaper Association of America are heartened by a key aspect of the pervasive effects of the Internet: the resurgence of language over graphics and symbolism in communications. There's a parallel resurgence in reading to get information, reversing the trend of simply watching and listening to information on TV. The Internet isn't a "talking lamp," as TV has been called. On the Net, the user is in an active conversation, the dynamics of which are constantly changing. The user has to be active, clicking and typing, to keep the conversation going. The Net is closer to direct advertising than other forms. Indeed, it's helping to revive direct advertising in print.

But the Net is still closer and more personal in its relationships to the user. **Tallying unique visits isn't enough: in more and more of the market information we see, there's a widening gap between site visits and commercial activity.** That's a bad sign for building brandwidth. As e-commerce develops, sales or click-throughs to sales will be a much better measure of the Net's effect. That's as it should be. Traffic is good, but it doesn't guarantee commerce any more than driving past a McDonald's guarantees buying a Big Mac. The speed of the Net also demands speed in developing relevance and hastens the perishability of the relevance you develop. You need to refresh it over and over again.

Better ways of measuring the results of noncommercial sites and the effect of advertising will be developed. We're big fans of Seth Godin, the innovative Net marketer, and his concept of "permission marketing." This is e-marketing that understands the nature of the medium and the relationship between the Web service and the consumer. It seeks to take that relationship far beyond awareness. Why judge a site on the basis of who saw it, rather than on what it DID to who saw it?

Web users come in every size and shape. Who's buying all that stuff on eBay.com? It's grandmothers, uncles, farmers, city folk, husbands, and wives. It's everybody. And the appeal has to be for all of them, but developed one at a time, personally. The great advantage is that you don't depend on discovery while driving around the neighborhood, just clicking around the Net—everybody can and does play. This is a general population getting more general all the time, as Net penetration grows. **These are the same folks, by the way, who are buying the shares that support the e-business revolution.**

Why is it that much advertising for Internet companies depicts the user as unidimensionally cool, young, and hip? It seems that the "liberation of creativity" in advertising has consistently been accompanied by the closing of advertising minds to the realities of the marketplace.

The Liberation of Creativity

In the late 1970s, the Coca-Cola Company was in deep trouble, and McCann-Erickson brought in a very avant-garde creative group to help develop new thinking on the account. Coca-Cola and its agency were busy making love to the hearts and minds of America and the world, and consumers told researchers they loved the brand. One little problem: They weren't buying it. They weren't translating their affection into transaction. The agency's solution was to bring in "new creative blood." These creative people had done breakthrough work in television advertising, and Coca-Cola anxiously awaited their concepts. At the time, Coke advertising was typified by warm and tender "Happy Valley" situations. Kids on a farm. Mom and Pop and Gramps and Sis and Bobby.

When the creative team presented their work it was shocking: it was the same old Mom and Pop and Gramps and Sis and Bobby.

"What's this?" we asked.

"It's Coke advertising," they answered.

For Coke, they had decided, you do Coke advertising. We wanted new, but got refried beans. They assumed this is what people expect of Coke advertising, particularly people at the Coca-Cola Company.

Today ad people undoubtedly feel the same way about Net advertising—this is what you do; the irreverent, edgy, and hip. The true liberation of creativity on the Net will be seen in advertising that builds on the fundamentals the way the best sites and services have done. That means advertising that does the basics, and then some.

Back to Basics

What advertising and all other forms of tactical marketing need to do now is what they were always supposed to do. They must inform and explain to consumers why they should move from one

**site to another. It's not about breaking rules. It's not about gratify-
ing the self-image of young entrepreneurs. It's about selling stuff.**

If it's true that, as Ogilvy said, clients get the advertising they deserve, we want e-businesses to deserve a lot better advertising, PR, and promotions. They certainly need the best performance, the serious-minded approaches that bricks-and-mortar companies some-times get and increasingly demand (consider Procter & Gamble's recent announcement that they are going to pay their ad agencies on the basis of performance). But too often they're not demanding it. They're asking for just the opposite—for more advertising with a nose ring. They figure if it's cool, it will be relevant. Wrong.

Winning awards is certainly no longer enough. None of that will help performance, and we need performance faster than ever before. The new entrepreneurs are very smart. They're also very ambitious. They aren't going to be satisfied with tactical marketing that doesn't create results, even by the advertising standard of delivering eye-balls. We find ad agencies shocked and amazed by the sudden disaf-fection of their Internet clients. One day the client doesn't come by for the cappuccino. Instead, they ring the agency: "We need a new campaign."

"But you loved those ads!"

"We were wrong. They didn't work," comes the response.

And the search begins for a new campaign and probably a new agency. With the same impatience with which they hired the agency after one cup of cappuccino and approved the campaign in record time, they pull the plug. The word is spreading: The Net needs results. Gulp.

**As the competitive crowd continues to grow, the e-entrepre-
neurs will recognize the need for marketing messages that are
highly relevant to consumers and clearly differentiated from
those of competitors.** They're going to look for ways to make sure consumers know exactly who they are, where they fit into their lives, and what makes them better than anybody else in the marketplace.

In other words, they'll be looking for the basics in every tactical application of their marketing messages.

They're going to learn to build brandwidth. The hard sell will hit the Net—indeed, if you look at the landgrab sweepstakes at Iwon.com, it's already hit. Hard sell is the opposite of lazy marketing. It doesn't just WORK hard; it's also hard to do. It rolls its sleeves up and works up a sweat. It's no different in the world of clicks than in the world of bricks and mortar. The job just keeps getting tougher. When *The End of Marketing As We Know It* was published, it was available on Amazon.com, of course. But within weeks, it was also available on Books.com, KingBooks.com, Borders.com, BarnesandNoble.com, FatBrain.com, Powels.com, Booksamillion.com, ComputerLibrary.com, and Booksnow.com. Half of them we hadn't even heard of before. Amazon.com's space has gotten very, very crowded. And as Amazon continues to expand what it sells into more and more categories, its brandwidth will be harder to define in its original category. By the time this new book has been on the shelves (shelves??) for a few weeks, there will be twenty more booksellers in the market. Prices won't be the innovation—everybody will be forced to meet the lowest prices. New "see you"s and "raise you"s will have to be developed in the book business, and they'll have to be communicated in new ways.

It's the same or will be the same in every category of e-business. It's more crowded than a Hong Kong slum. There will be more and more similarity in the products offered, the pricing, and the positioning of these companies. It's a natural herding tendency. Barriers to entry are low and getting lower all the time. Right now you can hop over most of them.

In that gathering crowd, how are you going to distinguish your business? If it's going to be on the basis of price, you'd better be ready to hit the bottom like you dove off a 3-meter diving board into an empty pool. On sites like PriceScan.com, consumers can check the prices in your category instantly. On sites like Deja.com, they can see all the options in a category rated side by side. Why should a consumer go anywhere but to the lowest priced competitor? And if you keep telling them price is important, that's exactly where they'll go (marketing is education, after all).

The answer to that question will be provided by e-marketing— and only the best of it. Advertising will have to do a hell of a job. And it won't be easy. It won't be the most fun you can have with your clothes on anymore. It's business. It's about selling stuff and making money.

About time, we say.

e-Lessons:

- ◻ We're not attacking creativity. We want to promote it in all tactical marketing: advertising, PR, promotions, direct and customized marketing—everything. Create tactics that work really hard. That's as creative as you need to be. Create ideas with exceptional relevance to consumers, help guide them through the competitive crowd, engage, connect and sell them. Now THAT'S creative.
- ◻ To build brandwidth, go back to the fundamentals of e-business and ALL business. Define your brand clearly. Explain to consumers why they should come to your site—on their terms, not yours. Tell them what your site is going to do for them, and remind them why it's going to do it differently and better than anybody else anywhere. Aggressively communicate what your brand is all about. Precisely identify the target audience and understand their perceptions and attitudes. Carefully develop the imagery of the user, usage, the product, and its associations

on and off the Net. Talk to your audience in their own language. Don't let cuteness or an attempt at hipness get in the way. When in doubt, just say it clearly and directly.

☐ Do all that and you'll be leading the real creative revolution on the Internet. And it won't take a nose ring to do it.

6

MARKETING AT WARP SPEED

You remember the scene: Han Solo and Chewbaca at the controls of Han's rusty tub of an intergalactic cargo ship, a fleet of the Empire's finest X-fighters closing in behind them with laser blasters locked and loaded. Han's ship is lumbering along. "Go for warp speed, Chewy!" Zzzzz-onnnnggg! The starry void ahead at first freezes then blurs past them as they leave the X-fighters standing still behind.

e-Pinions.com was the Internet equivalent of Solo's cargo ship shifting into warp speed. Profiled in the *New York Times Magazine*, this *Consumer Reports* type of site went from concept to IPO in something like 90 days. You could see the Mach forces on the faces of the e-Pinions workers from that blastoff. Things have slowed significantly for them now, back down to merely Mach speed from warp speed. In Silicon Valley alone in the first quarter of 2000, an average of seven companies were being launched per week, at an average cost of $10 million each. Zzzzz-onnnnggg!

That's Internet speed. And on the Internet, speed wins. That's the given of competition on the Internet—competition for notice, for money, for buzz, for users, and for revenues. And it's got Internet entrepreneurs from the Valley to the Alley awake and at their battle stations twenty hours a day. **e-Marketing's job is to add value, and these days velocity is value.**

GETTING THERE FIRST

Speed can mean the speed of distributing an idea. *The End of Marketing As We Know It* brought Sergio a deluge of requests from the smallest companies, everyone from aluminum siding companies to car washes to enterprising litigators. So he hired Kara Behar (sister of the Internet entrepreneur Mike Gilfillan) and Jessica Zyman (also genetically predisposed to marketing) to launch zmarketing.com, the ultimate marketplace for marketing, providing automated tools to run marketing programs for ANY business. There are now 38, and soon there'll be 100, people working on making this destination all you ever need to succeed in marketing. Needless to say, this business model depended on the Net to make sense and to make scale. Zzzz-onnnng!

This pace is tough on most traditional marketing people. They're used to the relatively leisurely pace of "marketing as we knew it." They're used to annual brand planning. How about HOURLY? They're used to the two-hour, two-chablis lunch. LUNCH?? How about a midnight pizza at your desk? That's the reality of the Net. When your competition changes the market dialogue, you have to react instantly. Waiting just means waiting for the toast to burn— and you're the toast.

Getting there first has been the imperative of the Internet. The first-mover advantage is accepted as a key to market success on the Net. The real deal, though, is getting there RIGHT first. Among many other market leaders, Microsoft has seldom been first to market. They were beaten to it by Lotus 1-2-3 and Lotus Suite, by IBM's OS2, by Novell's WordPerfect, and by others. But they've almost always been the first one in the market to get it RIGHT. For the crew in Redmond, it's been dogged determination, constant improvement, and very, very aggressive marketing that have brought success. In other words, it's been total commitment to their strategic directions.

GETTING THERE WITH THE MOST

Nathan Bedford Forrest, the Confederate general, is famous for more than being Forrest Gump's namesake. He was a fabled field general who gave the advice "Get there firstest with the mostest." What most people remember about the advice is the "firstest," but the thing you should take away from it is the "mostest." Forrest was a radical in battle strategy of the time. In those days, the cavalry was called "the eyes of the infantry." Mobile cavalry forces would define the enemy line and its strength along that line by constant skirmishing—dashing in for an engagement, then dashing out again. Connecting the dots of skirmishes allowed battle planners to decide where the weakest point of the line would be for attack. Once the weak spot in the enemy line was identified, most generals would typically commit no more than 15% to 20% of their troops to an attack. Military strategy of the time was conservative, and it was believed that you should wager only the maximum you were willing to lose. This is where General Forrest radicalized strategy. Once his skirmishers identified the weak point in the enemy line, he committed his total forces to attack there. His greatest victories were achieved by this stunning, overwhelming blow against an enemy who had never expected or prepared for that kind of commitment.

"Firstest" is good, but "mostest" is the defining factor in e-market strategies. Belief in strategy and commitment of resources are what deliver the KO punch in any developing market on the Internet. It is pouring commitment into that one focused point of opportunity that wins, and wins early. Andy Warhol's theory that everyone is famous for 15 minutes suggests you should be willing to squeeze the accordion of your marketing resources and your integrated marketing communications plans (that's what Chapter 7 is all about) and narrow them into a shorter, more focused market attack. Wham! If you let a competitor make that move on you, you should lie down, because you're dead. M2, as we affectionately call zmarketing.com, will see plenty of competitors. It will survive only if we "see" them and constantly "raise" them.

e-Marketing is marketing done on the fly. Get used to it. But that doesn't mean it's marketing done with a skip and a jump over the basics. One type of this warp-speed marketing is cut-to-the-chase marketing, wherein tactical development comes before strategic development: "Hey, let's do some marketing!" This reminds us of Mickey Rooney and Judy Garland in the old MGM films: "Hey, let's put on a show!"

"Who's got time for strategy? Half our engineers have great ideas for what the ad should look like, anyway."

And, naturally, this marketing program looks like it was designed by a half-dozen engineers, which is to say in engineering terms it's very, very granular: lots and lots of geekspeak about features—and none about benefits. They cap off their advertising with a nice, obscure, insolent headline. "I'm not so sure we should say 'suck' in the headline, Brian."

The shortest distance between any two points—like where you are now and your marketing objectives—is a straight line. That's what strategy provides you. You can't take a shortcut around strategy in the name of speed. As Senator Phil Gramm of Texas has said,

"When you're going down the wrong road, the one thing you don't want to do is step on the gas."

It would be interesting to map the meandering between those two points (YOU ARE HERE and BUSINESS OBJECTIVES) by companies that let tactics drive their marketing. No matter how fast you wander, it's not as fast as moving straight along a line defined by strategy. Get the strategy wrong enough, and you have to go all the way back to "Go." In the Web business, this means having to go back to the well for more funding. This is like taking a two-minute pit stop on the last lap of the Indy 500. The simple fact is you'll go a lot faster with a strategy than without one. A supersonic jet doesn't fly better if the pilots skip a few points on the preflight checklist. Flying at Mach 2 into a mountain doesn't often achieve the objectives of the mission. Likewise, you can't eliminate the basic steps of marketing planning—the e-marketing checklists. Make sure you've taken all the basics into account:

E-MARKETING PLAN CHECKLIST

☑ **Destination:** Did you clearly define where this strategy is supposed to take your brand? Have you defined what success will be?

☑ **Objectives:** Are your e-marketing objectives clearly linked to your business objectives? Have you homed in on just two or three key objectives?

☑ **Targets:** Have you defined your marketing targets from the inside out, starting with your own employees, your market partners, your current customers, your own investors and friendly analysts, other investors and analysts, trade and business journalists, market prospects, and those who influence market decisions? The strategy you've defined must work for ALL these marketing targets.

☑ **Customer Benefit:** Have you defined the brand benefit that covers all of these audiences? Or have you defined specific benefits by audience group?

☑ **Strategy:** What's the plan to achieve your e-marketing objectives? What's the road map to your defined destination?

☑ **Tactics:** Finally, you get to do the ad. But you must define 360 degrees of tactics, to surround your targets with an integrated message.

BRAND PLAN CHECKLIST

☑ **Awareness:** How are you going to build awareness for your brand with key audiences? How are you going to activate it through usage and word-of-mouth "viral" marketing?

☑ **Relevance:** Where does the brand fit into the needs and desires of your marketing targets?

☑ **Differentiation:** What makes your brand different and better than the competition? Can you define it in terms of rational and emotional benefits, not just features?

☑ **Credibility:** What's your plan to develop credibility with your marketing targets? How will you define expectations? How will you overdeliver on those expectations? What's the plan to claim the satisfaction you deliver?

☑ **Imagery:** How will you define user, usage, product, and associative imagery for the brand?

☑ **Brand Positioning:** Given all of the above, what is the brand positioning? Where do you fit in the marketplace today and tomorrow?

You can rip through these checklists. But in developing strategy you can't neglect them. Avoiding them is not just stupid; it's suicidal.

"DID YOU EVER HAVE TO MAKE UP YOUR MIND?"

That's what the Lovin' Spoonful asked back in the 1960s. It's a really good question right now. As they say, perfection is the enemy of good. You can cook strategy only so long and then you've got to decide, "It's as good as we're going to get. Let's go."

If you've gone through the basic checklists, you're ready to decide. Sure, even under the best of conditions that decision is a gamble. And it would feel a whole lot better to have exposed your strategic or tactical ideas to market research before dropping them on the entire market. But who's got six to eight weeks to run comprehensive research? This press of time has brought political researchers like Mark Penn and Doug Schoen, Bill Clinton's pollsters, to the Internet. These researchers are accustomed to working under intense time pressure with drop-dead consequences (nobody's been successful in pushing back Election Day). They're used to designing and executing research and providing analysis in the shortest time possible. With an existing sample they think nothing of providing overnight polling. It's not so much their technique as their experience and attitude. And they're much more adept at the quick read of research than are traditional market research groups; again, it's an attitude mothered by the necessity of having to develop campaign strategy on a day-to-day basis.

Scramble. Run through the checklist. Then take off. And when Regis asks, "Is that your final answer?" you can say yes. The research doesn't stop with the development of the advertising. You must monitor perceptions and attitudes in the marketplace constantly to maintain your ability to move quickly if a change occurs, be it positive or negative. You've got to have the tripwires out on the perimeter of your strategy to signal any sneak attack by the enemy. The idea is to create e-marketing strategy that is, as Bear Bryant said about the kind of football players he liked, "mobile, agile and hostile."

GETTING BUY-IN

One of the slowest processes in the Internet space is getting internal "buy-in" to strategic or tactical plans. Yes, it seems convenient for getting quick decisions that there may be only four or five people in the entire company, rather than four or five layers of marketing bureaucracy. Still, in most e-companies, you can bet that all four or five will have their say on every detail, down to the nittiest and grittiest, of strategy and tactics. (Actually, they'll usually sign off on strategy faster than tactics, which is like buying a used car based on the kind of tires it has.) "Founder's syndrome" is naturally rampant among Internet companies. The founders are most often young, brilliant, stubborn (at least a dozen people will have told them they were crazy to start the company in the first place . . . "Nyah-nyah-nyah-nyah-nyah!"), and very superstitious: "If I don't control it, it will be totally out of control. This is MY company, MY vision, MY BABY!"

Screeeeeeeech! That's the sound of brakes slamming on the whole e-marketing development process.

"I think slide fourteen is all wrong."

"What's wrong with it?"

"Well . . . it should be in all caps."

"But what about the strategy itself?"

"And I've got a problem with slide twenty-two, too."

Screeeeeech!

We know more than one e-founder who will take any brand positioning, logo, ad, or PR release to the code developers for their okay. **If you read *The End of Marketing As We Know It*, we hope you constantly remind yourself, "I'm NOT the target market."** As the Internet has moved beyond its first early-adopter phase of development, it has moved past the propellerheads and on to the regular people. So judging according to YOUR tastes or the tastes of a bunch of your Internet peers is close to irrelevant. After hearing a CEO-founder state he didn't identify with the brand strategy, we began to ask him some questions.

"What's your favorite kind of car?"

"I don't have a favorite car."

"What's your favorite line of clothing?"

"I don't care about clothes."

"Running shoes?"

"Don't care."

"Favorite brand of anything?"

"I don't have favorite brands."

On it went. And he considered himself a typical brand consumer. Sure. He was brand immune, almost preference immune, which put him in a crowd of about one one-thousandth percent of the population. We know of a pretty successful ISP (Internet service provider) with SEVEN founders on the scene—founder's syndrome times seven! You guessed it: It takes exactly seven times longer to get strategy developed there as anywhere else.

With the importance of speed on the Internet, this internal marketing campaign, getting buy-in, may be the e-marketing manager's most important job. The essentials are to keep decision makers actively involved in the process from strategy development to tactical finish. Get buy-in in baby steps, and lots of them—no big reveals. And context each next decision on the last one: "Based on the strategy we agreed on," "Based on the brand-positioning we agreed on," etc.

HERDING GEESE

Then there's the issue of bringing along your suppliers faster, much faster than they've ever worked before. Ad and PR agencies are notoriously slow to move under even ideal conditions. Part of the problem is tradition and process. Part of it is a workforce spread too thinly over lengthy client lists. And part of it is what we call "playing the clock." It's like those great college basketball teams that can control the ball to run the clock down. All of the tactical marketing agencies (ad, PR, direct mail, promotions, guerilla marketing, event developers, etc.) have a unique sensitivity for who will make the final decision on their work and for when that decision must ultimately be made. Ad agencies probably play it best.

"Of course, we'll need to have the ad campaign to show at the annual sales meeting in October," the brand manager mentions.

And guess when the ad campaign will be delivered to the client for a decision? Just in time to shoot the commercials or shoot the catalogue photography or develop the PR campaign or get the booth ready or prepare the banner ads so they can be shown at the annual sales meeting in October. That's playing the clock. It forces the decision. It's pretty much the same with PR, promotions, and the rest of the agencies. For these suppliers this is a subterfuge built on the bad experience of having clients kill their favorite ideas. The brand managers find that being backed up against the hot pipes narrows their choices somewhat.

On the Internet these same suppliers don't get anything like that kind of cushion.

"We've bought a page in the *Wall Street Journal* next week," the Web CEO will announce.

Bingo. The ad WILL get done.

"We're launching on the first of the month and we need a big sweepstakes!"—or PR campaign, or direct mail effort, or any of a dozen tactical marketing efforts.

Like playing the clock, Net time does narrow your choices. You can't send the supplier back to the drawing board again and again. That's too bad. But it also brings out the frankness in you. And that's very good. At one time you may have said, "I like that concept, except I wonder if it could get a little more in about how our solution is more comprehensive than our competitor's" and then patiently waited three weeks, when you saw the next try, to get a little tougher. Now you'll say, "No. That's all wrong. We need to say this . . ."

Saying no is faster than saying maybe. So be brutally honest with your suppliers. Having an idea come back one more time takes long enough—don't let it come back THREE more times. The best solution is to narrow the choices of the suppliers and your own people by providing a clear, concise, but comprehensive creative brief before any tactical work is started. An example:

The Creative Brief:

✓ *What is the market problem we are addressing?*

✓ *What change could help?*

✓ *Who are we talking to?*

✓   *What do we know about them that helps?*

✓   *What is the brand positioning—and how can you make it the creative springboard?*

✓   *Why should they believe it (what are the rational and emotional benefits)?*

✓   *How do we close the sale?*

The Internet itself has proved the value of fluid interaction. This allows the service to satisfy and even delight its customers by more clearly understanding their wants and needs. The same thing is true of ad, PR, promotional, and guerrilla marketing agencies, but it's the client who has to develop the interactivity. Despite the fact that they're a very bad idea, agencies love the BIG REVEAL: the drumroll, the Seigfried and Roy mist, the curtain rising on their Great Biigggg IDEA! In e-marketing, you've got to break your suppliers and your own direct-reports of this bad habit. If you're going to push your suppliers unreasonably, you've got to help them unreasonably, too. That means constant—read "daily"—contact on the progress of the work. They'll resist. But you resist the resistance. Getting there first and RIGHT demands that of you.

I'VE GOT A SECRET

Because of the importance of getting there first and getting there right, many companies are fanatical about secrecy. But there's a problem with secrecy: it blinds you. If you ask a six-year-old to become invisible, she'll close her eyes. That's the problem with e-corporate secrecy—it closes the eyes of your planning group to what's going on in the marketplace.

You saw *Saving Private Ryan*. You saw the GIs crouching in the landing craft at dawn that June morning almost sixty years ago. The scene shows in graphic realism the decisive first few days of the Allied invasion of Europe at Normandy. Many people would cite the D-Day invasion of Europe as one of the best-kept secrets in military history, but in fact the invasion was no secret at all. The Allies spent months amassing their forces and the material of war in Great Britain. All this was open to German intelligence. The invasion was discussed openly. The only secrets were where and when. These were protected carefully and accompanied, as Churchill put it, by a "bodyguard of lies," a number of deceptions to confuse the Germans about the place and precise timing of the invasion. Even with these obfuscations, it was the overwhelming force of the invasion, the willingness to commit the "mostest" to the "fastest," that made it a success.

The Net's transparency is a problem. You can't test-market ideas on the Net with any hope of concealing them from your competitors. About the most you can hope to do is freeze them in place momentarily when you announce a new change. That's why "vaporware" has been so successful for so many companies, including, famously, Microsoft. Some prefer to call it "potential-ware," since it really announces an initiative early in its development, meaning, quite often, that your developers are going to start working on it right after you announce it in the keynote speech at Comdex.

The idea is to set the market table before dinner—to try to hold a space for a new product initiative by announcing it before it can be introduced. It's the opposite of corporate secrecy. And it often succeeds in getting the competition to begin to work around the space you've defined. Invariably, they'll spend a lot of time simply denying or condemning the idea. The downside of the Internet's youth is its immaturity. Eventually, though, they'll begin to sell against the announced product development.

So, if you announce an initiative, you'd better be prepared to start selling it hard from that moment on. Trying to keep a secret on the Net is like trying to hide an elephant in the bathroom. Developing planning for secrecy just slows the whole process. It's better to work with the Net's natural advantage of openness and make it an advantage to your developmental process. Announcing development early also puts the finish line in sight for your own organization—giving them a definite goal. We call this process "A-Day/ D-Day":

- ☐ Announce the Development (A-Day)
- ☐ Sell It Like Hell
- ☐ Gauge the Market Reaction
- ☐ Adjust and Refine
- ☐ Deliver (D-Day)

THINK FAST—THINK LIKE A KID

You've got to think fast to be fast and you've got to be faster than ever today, on or off the Net. Web entrepreneurs tend to be pretty young, but no matter what their physical age, all of them think young. Young is fast. And age provides only the advantage of experience, if you're willing to learn. So learn to think like a kid:

Kids are stupid. They don't know what they don't know. They think if they jump off the garage roof, they can fly. In normal times, they would break their leg doing that. But in the Internet age, they earn a hundred million dollars. They ask stupid questions, which is why they don't remain stupid. "Amy, put that down, or you'll break it!" They're more curious than careful. Sometimes this gets them into trouble—more often it gets them into learning.

Kids believe in the tooth fairy. Not only are they superoptimistic (yes, indeed, somewhere in that huge pile of horse crap there is a pony), they live on a different plain of reality. "Yes, I can" is the prevalent attitude among Net entrepreneurs. Kids have been raised on choice and change. They can sit there with the TV remote—click, click, click, click, click, click, click—believing there's something great just a click away. Don't bet they're wrong.

Kids keep asking, "Are we there yet?" Kids are notoriously impatient. They can't stand waiting. They want to cut in line. And once in the movies, they beg, "What's gonna happen NEXT, Mommy?" Grown-ups know you can't always expect instant gratification. Kids don't. And kids run Internet companies.

Kids hyperfocus. Watch a kid playing Nintendo. Watch a kid playing Nintendo for four hours. Watch a kid with dyslexia (a condition that seems to afflict every Internet entrepreneur on the planet) watching the pattern his untied shoelaces make—while you're yelling at him to tie the damned sneakers. These kids do very, very well in developing a product vision later on: it's clear, constant, fixed, but in a whole new pattern.

Kids say the darndest things. Excuse little Stephanie, she just can't help saying exactly what's on her mind. And in this new economy that saves soooo much time (this new economy is about the economy of time, B.S., energy, focus—everything, it seems, except capital). We used to say that all clients tell the truth, eventually. These Internet clients tell it immediately. And it's refreshing.

@   @   @

Kids often don't appreciate these advantages. Adult perspective can be useful. After all, you didn't really appreciate the value of toys (you used to blow them up with M-80s) until you had the Amex Platinum and the Sharper Image. **The main advantage the young have over the old in this economy is that their minds are unencumbered; knowing too much (and, especially, knowing it ALL) is a real disadvantage in a new and emerging economy.** Don't let your experience weigh you down. Way too many marketing people have the attitude, "Everything I needed to know about marketing I learned in my first job as a brand manager." Cutting off your brain from learning is like cutting it off from oxygen.

@ e-Lessons:

- □ "Get there first" (that happens to be the positioning line of one of Internet Capital Group's biggest successes, Breakaway Solutions). But don't forget to commit the "mostest" to being "firstest." The winner is the one who gets it RIGHT first.
- □ You can't circumvent the basics in the name of speed. The shortest distance between now and success is following the straight line of strategy. Don't forget to go through the e-marketing checklists.
- □ But hurry! Cut the delays and push the process—and yourself. The Net makes marketing processes faster by providing fluid interactivity. Use it to push your own e-marketing development, keeping your managers involved and buying in to your decisions all along the way. Do the same with your suppliers: Demand an active dialogue during tactical development.
- □ Use the A-Day/D-Day process to help pre-position your new developments in the marketplace.

☐ The advantage of youth on the Internet is the unencumbered mind. Streamline your own thinking by always being willing to learn something new. Your consumers change their minds quickly. They learn quickly. You have to adjust to them.

☐ The same is true for so many companies on the Web. They don't have a reason for being, so to appease the investors they start packing additional features that conflict with the DNA of the original idea. They create confusion and sameness in a multidimensional way, masterful confusion, and soon they are irrelevant. Look at all the drugstore-type sites . . . now what is the USP and the difference between PlanetRX.com and drkoop.com and CVS.com and on and on? Can't figure it out? The consumers can't, either. The fundamental premise that launched them got lost. Is the equity of drkoop.com being maximized? It doesn't look like it. It looks like the same unbranded site as all the rest. Can it be done? Absolutely, but you need to rethink and relaunch quick, or it's adios com.

7

BUILDING BRANDWIDTH MEANS BUILDING EVERYTHING

When you talk to most management people about marketing, what they're thinking about is just advertising. You could write a book about how frivolously people think about the important practice of marketing (a good title would be *The End of Marketing As We Know It*). **Obviously, you believe marketing is serious business, or you wouldn't have read this far. And you know marketing is a lot more than advertising. In fact, it's everything.**

Most people define marketing as a process meant to add value to transactions in a marketplace. All kinds of activities are part of that process:

□ First is the development of the product you take to market; this is the weightiest determinant of value. How does the product perform? How different is the product from other similar products in the marketplace?

□ Then there's the package. It, too, must perform and differentiate. It must help define the product; connect it to the wants, needs, and tastes of the market prospects; and, in doing so, enhance value.

☐ Then there's the price, a definer, but certainly not the last determinant of the value of the product.

☐ There's the distribution of the product in the marketplace; there's the promotion in the store, on the package, or through advertising; there's the advertising; there are the PR and IR (investor relations); there are the events and community activities sponsored in the name of the brand; there's the image of users in the marketplace; there's the image of how the product is used in the marketplace; there's the image of the companies and other institutions that are associated with the brand; there's the way the delivery trucks look; there's the way service personnel do their job; there's the way customers' problems are solved; there's the way the company has reacted to a crisis that spills into the marketplace news; there's often a well-known business figure associated with the company and/or brand, sometimes an endorser; there's the way people answer the phone at headquarters; there's the product warranty or guarantee.

☐ There are another fifty details, depending on the product and category.

Phew! All of those details will add value to the transaction, or, if done poorly, subtract from it. **Everything markets. It's the corollary to "everything communicates."** Every last detail of your operations, communications, and market interactions communicates to some important audience, whether you intend it to or not. Some details that add or subtract from your value, for instance, competitive activities or environmental changes in the marketplace, will be very hard for you to control. But you DO control your reaction to those uncontrollables. **Once you understand that everything communicates, you want to get control of as many of the details as** possible. That's why we always recommend developing one core marketing strategy around which all those details must be formed. To affect every one of the details listed above, marketing has to be in the very center of a company's operations. It's not that marketing has to run the business, but an element of marketing must be developed into every aspect of the business.

If you're a marketing person, get busy. If not, start thinking like one.

The idea of integrated marketing means making all the details work together, so that each of them enhances value and the whole of them enhances value more than the sum of the parts. "Blended marketing" might be a better description, so you think of marketing as a great recipe that stirs all of the elements together successfully. How often do you see a company or brand with truly integrated marketing? In fact, how often do any TWO elements of that big marketing mix actually coincide in strategy and tactical execution? Not often.

In larger companies, particularly in highly bureaucratic ones, almost every one of the elements of marketing is carried out by a separate group, under an isolated set of objectives and strategies. They don't talk to each other. They don't even WANT to talk to each other. In those companies, marketing has authority over advertising, promotion, and maybe packaging. Sales runs distribution and probably pricing. PR often reports directly to corporate affairs, because of the importance placed on communicating to shareholders and analysts. Who owns the giant inflatable of the product that's floating above the exhibition hall at trade shows? In fact, who owns trade shows? This results in anything but integrated, blended marketing. For fifty important details of marketing that add or subtract value, there will be fifty different cooks who aren't reading off the same recipe. The result: an unpalatable stew.

You walk into a store to see a product with a "value added" sweepstakes promotion developed by the marketing guys. Say, "Tide with 20% Blue Specks That Clean Faster." But just down the shelf is a deep discount dreamed up by the sales guys on another-sized package of the same product. And over on the newspaper rack you find a story about the CEO attracting an important brand-name board member. The discontinuity fuzzes the meaning of all three separate communications and cancels out any chance for synergy. It's a waste of money and a blown opportunity.

Read "e-marketing" as "everything-marketing." Recognize that everything markets, and everything markets more effectively when it's integrated and driven by one central strategy and objectives that are the same as the business objectives. All marketing people should work this way, but they don't. Think how much more productive marketing in most companies, online or off, would be if it were truly "everything marketing." It's enough to scare the pants off Alan Greenspan.

In smaller companies and Net startups, more of the total marketing mix is put into fewer bosses' hands. That's a step in the right direction, though it's usually unintentional. They don't really understand the value gained by adding marketing strategy to every aspect of operations and communications. It won't help that if the startup grows, it'll start departmentalizing and the bosses will compartmentalize the marketing process. And they'll probably start thinking of the "marketing person" as the person who does the ads. A great leap backwards.

It helps if the CEO has a good sense of the importance of marketing—if he's Steve Jobs, for instance, or Steve Case. If you're a CEO, it's good news that you're reading a book like this. **If you're a marketing person, the most important selling you'll ever do in your life will be to convince your boss that marketing should be integrated into every aspect of the company's endeavors and all of marketing should be integrated.**

SURROUND YOUR TARGETS

The reason for this effort to blend all the details of marketing together is to control the messages about your brand that reach every audience in any situation at any time. Where will they get their lasting impressions of your brand? From product experience? From the distinctive packaging or apt logo design? From the way you stand by your guarantee or help them with a problem? Which detail will be most important? You never know. Most often, it is the total effect of ALL the details that builds the brand and the brand value. You want control of the effect everywhere consumers turn. This means surrounding them with your messages in every way: content, tone and attitude, communicated values, etc. We know a smart retailer marketing manager who describes it this way: "We want to create a box around the prospect. Anywhere they look, they see something about us that's meaningful."

The press has reported Jeff Bezos of Amazon.com as saying that his company's mission is to be the most "customer-centric company in the universe." So who's writing their press releases? All the press releases talk about is the next line of business they're opening up, the next patent they're suing to protect, the next world they intend to conquer. Why aren't they talking about customers?

Most Web companies communicate one message to Wall Street and another to their customers. Most of them communicate almost not at all to their own employees. But all of the audiences in your communications ecosystem will be tuned to messages from and about your brand. If these messages are inconsistent, they'll be assimilated inconsistently by those audiences. Surrounding your marketing targets isn't about just filling the air with noise about your company. It's about developing a consistent set of themes and messages that replay every time your customers see mention of the brand. **You can't assume that you'll be able to rope off one**

audience from information targeted at another. It's remarkable how many consumers today are reading business news with frequency and sophistication. For years there was an assumption that consumers' mood would affect the stock market. Now that's working in reverse. **Assume that everybody is going to see everything.**

CREATE LAYER-CAKE COMMUNICATIONS

Like we said, truly integrated marketing communications campaigns are blended like a great recipe. Think of a thick, rich layer cake. The advertising is the icing. That's about what it should be in importance. But the layers of the cake must blend together: the PR campaign, the customer relationship management, 800-number support lines, events you sponsor, graphic design, internal company and shareholder communications . . . Layer after layer, they have to work together to develop the total brand story. Every layer, in fact, every crumb must help make that brand story better, richer, thicker.

Every molecule of marketing communications has to be doing what the whole process is doing: helping to define the brand, connect marketing targets to it, and enhance value.

You've seen media planning flow charts. Generally, they're devised to make sure your message is never out of view of your marketing targets. After the TV spots go off the air, the radio fills in, the print advertising kicks in, and so on. **In today's environment, though, delivering and sustaining your messaging are jobs that must be carried far beyond advertising.** That flow chart must include every detail of communications. What are our customers going to think when they use our product? What will the package communicate? And on and on. This layering builds brandwidth.

You've also got to think in terms of delivering the messaging in blasts calculated to cut through all the market noise, all the clamor of buzz and competitive claims. So plan to develop many communications events on top of one another: ads, PR, IR, events and sponsorships, new promotions, new packaging, new product developments. Create the highest decibel level, but make sure it's all playing the same tune. The first priority should be effect, not efficiency. Sustaining a message that never got through in the first place is just plain stupid. **Better two or three big marketing blasts than nine months of market mumbling. Roll the dice. If you did your homework, you'll be a winner.**

No angel or venture capitalist is going to provide you with enough cash to pull along your total brand plan on one tactic alone, advertising or PR or one cool promotion. That's way too inefficient and wasteful. You need EVERYTHING communicating for your brand. And you need all of it working together.

The first place to look for more pulling power is to PR, what we call "earned media." This is the most ineffectively used aspect of marketing communications in companies, big and small, online and offline.

PR: WILL IT BE YOUR WATERLOO?

In America, most traditional marketers have gotten very lazy. With huge resources and an acceptance of the idea of mass marketing, too many of them get away with remarkably wasteful marketing, blasting away at the market with very expensive shotgun shell after shotgun shell of advertising campaigns. The lack of a solid PR strategy is often the loss of the nail that creates the loss of a shoe that creates the loss of a horse that creates the loss of a king that creates the loss of a kingdom. **Companies and brands almost always die of unnatural causes, untimely deaths, smothered under an avalanche of bad news and bad timing.** Negative information far outweighed positive, and the company eventually toppled over. It could have been avoided. But marketers are too lazy to shore it up.

Indeed, most marketers don't even think of PR as marketing.

Most big marketers have come to rely on the most visible and least credible of all communications media: broadcast TV. Yankelovich Research reminds us that network TV advertising has a credibility level of about 6%, meaning that 94 cents of every advertising dollar goes down the tubes.

It's Barcalounger marketing: totally lazy. Most big marketers today leave undeveloped one of the most important strategic marketing tools: PR. We realize it was PR agencies that gave PR a bad name in the first place, for practicing "PR by the pound": they waste tons of perfectly good paper for press releases without focus or meaning or effect, except to while away the PR minions' day. Then, too, it was never seeing the PR bigshot again after the pitch meeting. PR has earned itself a bad name, but that doesn't diminish its importance.

PR is important because it creates third-party validation of your messages by news media. It helps generate marketplace buzz, and that's a hell of a lot more convincing than advertising. If broadcast TV ads have a 6% level of credibility, word-of-mouth testimonials must have about an 80% level of credibility, and those testimonials are often generated by what's seen, heard, or read in the news. In political campaigns, PR is essential. It's called "free media," and it's often the most relevant messaging a campaign will do: issue positions and white papers, speeches, debates, campaign coverage, schmoozing with reporters on Air Force One. Key themes and messages of a campaign are usually established in the free media—our colleague David Morey correctly renamed this "earned media"—and backed up in the paid media, or advertising. The communications person for a political campaign is a pretty pure marketer, running some of the most integrated communications campaigns in the world. Spin is just as hard and important on the

Internet (and in Internet finance) as it is in any campaign. It's just as hard and important in ALL of marketing.

Remember the political principle of "do the doable." Politics, at least before the days of Johnnie Chung and the Clinton money machine, has been about conservation of resources. You focus on only that which you're pretty sure you can get done. And PR is very useful and efficient in that equation.

THE MAKING OF MARCOMM

Many high tech companies have a tradition of using PR as the core element of marketing. The PR industry on the West Coast mostly grew up alongside high tech companies. PR focused on the unending march of new product introductions and upgrades was the most effective way to communicate to core users, who avidly read the buff books.

It was felt that PR could cover the product issues much more effectively than advertising could, particularly with the defined marketing targets of most high tech companies, the influential and sophisticated end users of technology. Product reviews were (and still are) hugely important in high tech to get the early adopter experts and generate word of mouth. So spin is just as important here as in politics. Media relations, the handling and fondling of influential journalists, is an art in itself and key to the success of any PR campaign.

The marketing department in most high tech firms is called "MarComm," for "marketing communications," indicating that PR is the lead messaging tool. That's not to say this tool is used properly all or even part of the time by Internet companies. Most startups focus PR primarily on the Wall Street analysts and investors. And much of this PR is pure, old-fashioned ballyhoo.

Good PR has to have the discipline of focused brand communications. It must be integrated into all other communications, from Web site to advertising. Otherwise, it disappears into the ether. PR must be used in a highly targeted way. It must develop the same five key components of brand strength that are developed in other communications. It must be highly creative to be highly effective. And it should get the devotion of resources to make it work. Indeed, as we said, at a lot of high tech companies, advertising is used only to support PR, not as the mainstream marketing medium. The typical MarComm department has put PR at the center of its marketing communications and built around it with sales promotion, events (such as user group events), community activities, and internal communications.

MAKING THE CEO LOOK GOOD

PR is an afterthought in the typical mass marketing campaigns of many companies. These companies have put PR into the category of "corporate communications," which is just another phrase for "communications to make our corporation look good" and, quite often, "communications to make our CEO look good." You'll almost always find "corporate communications" people reporting directly to the CEO or chair of these firms. The communications are almost always focused on investors and analysts, the people who can REALLY make a CEO look good. These CEO-focused departments become adept at the CEO-stroke, and these CEOs measure the ink devoted to them in quantity, not quality. A photo op, of course, is considered a coup de grace. If anybody ever practiced Tom Peters's principle of "the brand of me," it's these CEOs (though we know this isn't what Peters had in mind). This stuff really wears out its welcome with the press. "You call this news?"

And it takes a lot of time, effort, and money to generate diddly. This stuff was symbolized by the CEO preening in *Barbarians at the Gate,* typical of the 1980s leverage buyout cowboys in particular (a great many of whom were what real cowboys describe as "all hat, no cattle"). And we still see a good bit of it around today with Internet CEOs.

Yes, the CEO has a role in PR—but self-congratulation isn't it. What it is, defining the future, we'll talk about later in this chapter. At best, you might consider the CEO-strokes corporate communications as IR. There's nothing wrong with IR; it's important in any public company, but it should be just one part of a total PR campaign.

DEVELOPING THE INTEGRATED PR CAMPAIGN

Even if you've got a huge commitment to advertising, you can't ignore the need for an integrated, strategic PR campaign. **PR should achieve the same brand objectives as advertising or any other marketing communications: building presence, relevance, differentiation, credibility, and brand imagery.** But the focus of the PR campaign should be on the three Ds:

- □ Define the brand.
- □ Define the company.
- □ Define the future.

These are issues that tell the total story of the enterprise, the brand, products or services, the competitive set, and the customer. **Although PR tactics often begin in print, the idea is to generate talk: a buzz.** PR tells a story with a beginning, middle, and end, a destiny and outcome. It establishes a story line that can be repeated easily and even embellished as it branches out through the viral net-work, person to person. That story line can be contracted (yelled into the closing elevator door) or expanded (told over glasses of wine on a flight to Tokyo). It tells a story that often relates to a cate-gory of stories that have been told in the past, just as so many time-less fairy tales share four or five themes; this makes them easier to remember and relate. This is certainly true in the business press, where the same handful of stories circulate.

Butch Cassidy
There's what we call the "Butch Cassidy" stories, about the little or little-known company that comes out of the pack to success: "Who *are* those guys?"

Little Big Brand
There's a closely related set of stories about little-known companies that associate with bigger, better known brands: "What does [the leader brand] know that you [emerging brand] don't know?"

Lost Sheep
There are the "lost sheep" stories for the companies that have gone off the market tracks, having lost focus on their core objectives or core competence. Often, these stories are written by journalists who are saying "I told you so" about the company or about the principle involved.

Back to Basics
There's a set of "back to basics" stories about companies regaining that focus on the key factors that led to their success (after being "lost sheep"). Virtually every corporate turnaround is written about in the business press from this perspective.

Whatever Happened to . . . ?

Then there's the "whatever happened to . . ." stories that refer to a formerly well-known company, brand, or individual and highlight the journalist's homework capability, but also fit into a very readable category of corporate stories.

@   @   @

Good PR is good storytelling. Good PR helps construct the good (interesting, credible, and compelling) story and place it in motion. At different times and in different media, the story will highlight each of the classic questions of news reporting: Who? What? Where? When? Why? In this way, the best PR helps shape the story once it's in motion.

Good advertising is often about associating imagery with an idea (think of Nike and athleticism). It is time and space compressed, after all, and you can't do a whole lot more than that. Sometimes it associates a brand with a simple concept ("Look, Ma. No cavities!"). On rare occasions, it tells a complete story ("I told you Priceline.com was going to be big . . . REALLY big!").

Let's look a little closer at those three key stories that PR tells.

Defining the Brand

PR tells the brand story. What is this thing (product or service)? What does it do? Why was it developed? Who, what, where, when, and why? Where does it fit in people's lives (relevance)? What makes it different from the competitive set (differentiation)? How has it proved its market claims (credibility)? What symbols, images, or icons can be associated with this brand (user, usage, product, and associative imagery)? It may take more than one PR effort, more than one story, to answer all these brand questions. If so, a number of individual events, releases, interviews, etc. must be coordinated to do the total job, one part at a time.

In defining the brand, PR follows the brand strategy, adapting tactics to its particular means and media. Telling the brand story means telling the product story. But in e-marketing the "gee whiz!" product stories have lost their appeal to an audience of press people and consumers who are less and less surprised by any new development: "You mean this thing will make my PC fly? Whatever."

So the product description just doesn't cut it anymore. There must be more to the story than performance dynamics and product attributes. Remember, there are 800 million stories out there on the Worldwide Web. **Certainly, the story must communicate things from a user perspective. What are the consumer benefits?** But unless you've bought a couple hundred pages of advertising in the same magazine, there'd better be more to the story than that.

What we've learned is the need to create branding events: focal points of interest that help propel the brand story; puzzle pieces of information that, when put together, tell the greater brand story. Branding events are about content and substance, not sizzle or spin. They are moments that help you attach the brand to the story (one of those five key themes in the business press, for instance) and make it yours.

Telling the brand story is the most important job of PR for any kind of product or service on or off the Net.

We learned an important but painful lesson working in politics: if you don't define yourself clearly and quickly, your opponent will do it for you. This has happened often in politics, usually to the lesser-known candidate running against a better-known incumbent. An example was Governor Michael Dukakis, the unknown but attractive Democratic candidate for president in 1988. Early in the campaign he was riding on top of the "bubble," as it is called in politics, a bubble of popularity based mainly on the new face in the race, with none of the known faults of the incumbent. Dukakis rode this bubble past the Democratic primaries and the nomination. He was the young governor of a booming state, seemingly full of new ideas and energy. But that was about all anybody knew of him.

Being the popular but almost unknown choice of a majority of voters is a tricky challenge. But it can be overcome. In 1992, this was Clinton's position. In the successful cases, the campaign manages to build a structure of biographical, issue, and character substance beneath the candidate to replace the bubble when it inevitably bursts. When the challenge is not overcome—the Dukakis case was a spectacular example—the candidate never has a chance to fill in the details. In 1988, that was done for Dukakis by Roger Ailes, Vice President Bush's brilliant campaign strategist, now head of Fox News. The Republicans began right after their nominating convention with negative TV spots supplying disturbing facts about Dukakis and saying, in effect, "Do you really know this guy?" They depicted him as an extreme liberal ("card-carrying member of the Americans for Civil Liberties"), soft on crime ("Willie Horton"), soft on defense ("the tank"), and failing to deliver on his own liberal principles ("Boston Harbor"). Dukakis refused to respond to the attack. He played "rope-a-dope," as Muhammad Ali did in his famous "Rumble in the Jungle" championship fight against young George Foreman, leaning on the ropes, taking Foreman's best punches, letting the younger man exhaust himself, before springing into action and pummeling him. For the great Ali, it worked (though these poundings surely had lasting effects on his health and well-being). Dukakis hoped Ailes and Bush would run out of ammo. The problem with rope-a-dope is the damage you sustain on the ropes, taking those punches. By the time Dukakis tried to spring into action, there was no spring left: he was out cold in a TKO.

We've seen many a corporation try this same tactic out of panic in a crisis or out of that incredible stupidity called "acting like a leader," which most often means "not dignifying the attack" or "not giving our competition free mention in the press." It means taking 15 or 16 roundhouse shots to the head before even forming a defense. **And the best defense is the one formed before your opponent even goes on the attack** (more on this later in the chapter, when we talk about crisis communications).

Define your brand, or somebody else will define it for you: It may be a political or consumer activist with a very rusty axe to grind; a broker interested in shorting your stock; an opportunistic market competitor; or an exhausted, overworked reporter, mainlining Starbucks Arabica, too harried to do thorough or objective market research.

Defining the Company

Defining the company comes after the brand has been defined—often as a result of success in defining the brand. "Who ARE those guys?" **It means defining the culture, strategy, and individual contributions that could create the successful brand.** The company may be seen as technologically superior/aggressive/vision or values driven/modern or traditional in approach, strategy, and structure.

As we've said, the ideal situation is for the success of the brand and brand story to spark curiosity in journalists and consumers about the company story. (Think of Ben and Jerry's.) In this case, the company story must convince the audience that this brand could only have been created by the unique dynamics existing at this company. The brand and company should be seen as fraternal twins—extensions of the same gene pool. Naturally, defining the company well is terribly important to both IR and human relations and recruiting. **The buzz on the company among analysts and investors must be developed to make your own investors look smart enough to recognize the inevitability of success.**

It's the defining of the company that will make it possible to retain and recruit the best people. The best people can get rich anywhere. They want to be able to identify with a compelling story, a professed market or product vision, a cool company.

Defining the Future

Defining the future is a suitable role for the CEO and in many ways his or her most important communications job. This forms the outline of the CEO's basic stump speech (a political term taken from Honest Abe's standing on a tree stump to be seen and heard better). In politics, the stump speech is the basic speech of the campaign. It carries all the key themes and messages of the candidate and his or her competitive strategy. It can be delivered formally from a podium or very informally in a personal conversation. It can be delivered in five minutes or an hour and a half. But the form and substance of this stump speech do not vary. The speech is altered (usually at the beginning) only to adapt to the situation at hand ("It's sure good to be here in Kansas City") or perhaps to emphasize one set of issues over another, given the situation at hand ("And I know how you folks feel about the American family farmer").

The CEO needs a basic stump speech as much as the political leader. It carries the brand story and the company story, of course, but it must carry more. It must establish a context for the brand and company in the lives of its listeners. The most interesting context is always the future:

☐ What listeners' lives will be like in the future—usually described in Mr. Wizard's optimistic terms, but sometimes described as a dark "what if?"

☐ How your brand will fit into their lives.

☐ Where other products and other categories of products will have evolved to and what product developments will be coming along from your company.

☐ What obstacles exist to that rosy tomorrow and how listeners can help lower them.

Defining the future clearly describes the destiny of your company and brand. It clearly tells your employees, partners, investors, customers, and competitors who you are and will be, what values you believe will take you to success, what kind of role you project for your brand in people's lives—in short, your corporate vision. So it can be inspiring for your own constituents and confining to your competitors (positioning the other guy is just as important as positioning yourself).

Defining the future projects your company as a success. It projects the growing importance of your ideas and brands into the future. Bill Gates has always projected Microsoft's stated corporate mission: "A computer on every desk, in every home" (And, aw shucks, folks, we don't even make computers). It creates the image of success toward which your people can work.

People don't necessarily become great seers of the future just because they become CEO. Obviously, there are other traits of management leadership that are important. Usually this "defining the future" capability is taught. We work with CEOs in what we call "candidate training," the same rigorous training through which we put our political candidates. Like all good conditioning, "candidate training" is meant to establish a form that can stand up to any situation and repel attack. We develop the brand, company, and future stories. We practice them in formal and informal situations. We simulate the press conference full of attacking reporters, peppering the CEO with leading and aggressive questions under harsh, hot lights, and teach him or her what every successful political leader knows: you never have to answer the question asked; you can simply use it as a launch pad for the answer you want to give. The CEO should never experience a situation that's tougher than the one he or she encounters in this training. This is the camp le jeune of the CEO's main communications job, defining the future.

ADDING MORE AND MORE BRANDWIDTH

In the spirit of "do the doable," good PR is good at target selection. Mass messages are as ineffective in PR as they are in advertising. The key to successful messaging is to clearly understand the target and the medium. Targeting key constituents for your PR messages, just as with advertising, means understanding demographics and psychographics, but also understanding attitudes toward key issues related to your brands and company. Knowing this information allows you to develop content and a delivery system or a media plan for the themes and messages of your brand, company and definition of the future stories. The idea is to select a number of different distribution means for information (ads, merchandising, promotion, PR, IR, direct or customized communications, events and sponsorships, word of mouth, etc.) and use them all. Don't let anybody miss any of the elements of your story or your retelling of the same story in another form, chapter, or medium. This is the way you seep into people's thinking and talking. This is the way buzz is created and sustained as it ricochets off the walls of that information box.

Most dot.coms have a wide array of communications targets: their own employees, their investors, Wall Street analysts, trade and business journalists, potential employee recruits, market partners, customers, and sometimes even the competition. In the best PR campaigns—such as Commerce One's integrated strategy to develop and then communicate its MarketSite concept with General

Motors—those targets are hit from every angle, through every medium, from electronic press releases to PowerPoint shows to word of mouth.

MAKING IT HAPPEN

PR is not just press releases! (Even though they are the commodity of the PR industry and its bane, as the three-martini lunch used to be the image of the ad industry.) **PR is brand strategy told in story form in nonpaid media, in EARNED media.** So, indeed, PR is a lot more than press; it's people. Too many dot.coms judged their PR by the poundage of press releases. That's naive. Press events are met with the kind of cynicism that TV advertising slams into: What your communication targets believe is what they hear from their peers, or think they remember hearing from their peers.

Most PR happens the way the bumper sticker tells us: "S––t Happens." That is, most of it is unexpected and bad. What's black and white and red all over? The surprise newspaper story that makes your brand bleed to death.

Developing successful PR is a matter of careful planning and flawless execution. There's a checklist we go through with Z Group or Core Strategy Group clients:

Successful PR means successful strategy. Everything starts with strategy, with a clear road map forward. Far too much PR is done ad hoc. It's a matter of whim, or it's attached to events over which it has control, or it's formed in the headlights of oncoming competitive traffic. Success means developing strategy—developing the story lines for company, brand, and CEO and relating all of them into a whole. Since April 2000, dot.coms have gotten a lot more strategy-friendly, but still too few of them demand a strategic foundation before building their PR campaigns. And seldom are these strategies developed by PR agencies, online or offline. This is your job, e-marketing manager: to provide the strategic compass for all marketing communications.

Make it happen. Good PR isn't about reporting corporate and brand events over which it has no control. Instead, it is about forming, aligning, and strategizing these events. PR strategy should work closely with the development of business strategy. It's a more constant voice and constant information source of the brand or company's development than are ads and other paid marketing communications, which come in spurts. The PR strategy will influence the timing and definition of key company and brand issues— by a new product introduction or product feature development, new marketing campaigns, and corporate events and sponsorships. **Successful PR doesn't wait—it takes control.** It plans. The success of Commerce One's PR strategy to announce its MarketSite partnership with General Motors was in the planning. It seemed that every detail was thought through: There was Commerce One's CEO in the appropriate pin-stripe suit and rep tie, and there was GM's CEO in Friday casuals, no tie, sport shirt unbuttoned.

Create a calendar of action. Our good friend Hamilton Jordan is one of the most talented strategic organizers in or out of politics. He engineered Jimmy Carter's outsider campaign for the presidency in 1976. Later, with Carter out of office and his reputation in a shambles, Hamilton engineered Carter's return to a position of respect and admiration. Hamilton entered any political campaign meeting room carrying under his arm huge white boards that displayed intricate timelines drawn in thick magic marker—every day from now until election day. Now there are PowerPoint presentations, Lotus Notes calendars, and a host of project management tools that can put those displays in the palm of your hand.

For the corporate world, election day is the date by which company objectives must be achieved. On these timelines, Jordan lists known events that will take place in the coming months: Known events are those over which the company has complete control or some shaping control. He lists potential unknown events (government activities, competitive threats, product or brand breakdowns), over which the company has little control. And he forces the strategy group to begin to develop the 12-month calendar of events that will define the brand story, the company story, and the story of the future, as seen by the CEO. This last calendar defines the way in which the company will get its story into motion and into the minds of its key targets.

Focus on the "Big Mouths." John Scanlon, the pioneer PR strategist, came up with the idea of the "Big Mouth" list. This is a list of the people who can influence the thinking of your core communications targets. This list goes beyond, for example, Microsoft's targeting of "influential end users" to the opinion leaders they read, listen to, or hear about. Scanlon recognizes that you can't simply give these "Big Mouths" a script. Their objectivity is what gives them credibility. Though some of them may be friendly to your cause, you create a calendar of messaging and information events meant to provide them with information and opinion that support your story. This strategy must be carried out over a long time; it takes a while to shape opinion or even to activate the opinion of those who may support you. But it's key to building momentum for your story, for your side of the market arguments. We never develop a communications strategy for a dot.com without understanding this terribly important medium of communication and testing the themes and messages we'll be trying to send through it.

Underpromise and overdeliver. Here's the communications formula for developing customer satisfaction: Define Expectations +

Overdeliver on Them + Claim Credit. This applies to PR as much as to any other marketing communications. But PR is generally as guilty as advertising of violating the formula. Overpromise and underdeliver is the rule. That's because the PR manager is looking for a successful press conference, not a successful execution of a long-term strategy. That successful press conference is inflated with corporate puffery. It's what we call "teeing up the brand": To provide the energy of positive spin, the company uses wild hyperbole (on the theory that the press will never be quite as enthusiastic as you are, so PUMP IT UP), with the result that the brand promise is placed on a tee—just waiting for events and cynical journalists to drive it into the woods. As we said earlier, in Internet reporting, the "OhmyGod" product developments have made most journalists and business or consumer targets less sensitive to product news. This idea of the "great press conference" sets up the brand or company or CEO for failure in the future. Don't set unreachable expectations. Don't depend too greatly on the naivete or amnesia of media and business professionals. Set reasonable, doable expectations. Let the press conference become brilliant later on, when those expectations are exceeded and you claim credit.

Communicate inside out. We learned in politics the importance of communicating PR campaigns inside out. Before you can communicate successfully outside, you must first communicate to your own team, your own paid employees, your own volunteers, your own loyal supporters. A good inside-out campaign gains strength as it moves outward from the candidate and management to employees, partners, shareholders, and core customers. In working with Coca-Cola issues over the years, we developed an important principle of communications: "Sell the system; the system will sell the Coke." That means that the brand story, company story, and definition of the future must be told first to employees, then to the distribution system and its employees, then to retail and fountain customers, then to market partners and co-promoters and their employees, and then to the brand's most loyal customers. Do all that well, and you're guaranteed success. They'll do the selling for you. Indeed, these people provide the most important and compelling medium of advertising that exists. They can become the disciples who will spread your word and gather converts.

Communicating inside out also follows the principle of surrounding your core communications targets. They begin to hear more and more voices, speaking as evangelists of your brand. It means preaching to the converted. Contrary to popular opinion, that's not a bad idea—it's a brilliant one. This is the communications strategy of the evangelical church. **Yes, you should preach to the choir. You must teach them the words to the hymns.** You must energize them to march out the doors of the church and become missionaries. Nobody sells anything better. After the mind-numbing fall of the NASDAQ in spring 2000, all Net companies have to think hard about employee motivation and retention. Employees are not only the first layer of inside-out communications, but probably the most important one.

Ground the PR campaign. Yes, the glowing article on page 1 of the business section is great stuff. It shines down on every communications target, from the inside to the outside. **But successful PR campaigns are built from the ground up, not from the sky down. Great PR creates a foundation of market talk and market talkers.** The story lines move out virally in every direction. It's harder to lay this groundwire of communications—ask Qwest what it was like to lay fifteen thousand miles of fiber cable—but it's the necessary infrastructure of PR success. The groundwire is the result of the little things—the little events, the precise targeting of influential Big Mouths, the introduction of repetitive news into the market along an event-filled calendar.

WHEN CRISIS HITS

Every company and every brand will have a crisis. It may be an attack by government regulators or aggressive competitors. It may be a self-inflicted wound from corporate missteps. But . . . kiss the Book . . . it will happen to you.

We've seen it again and again. Suddenly, employees notice that management's doors are slamming shut. There are rushed, hushed meetings going on. Nothing is said outside the doors. Lawyers have instructed the management to not say anything about the issue. Managers may be suffering paralysis, uncertain what to do next. Or they may have made the typical corporate decision not to "dignify" the attack of an opponent. They stonewall. The loudest noise is the incessant sound of employees whispering, supplying with rumor what's been left out by management communications. And so, no matter what the root cause, the crisis deepens.

Don't form a crisis management team. At this point many managers make the cardinal mistake of forming a "crisis management team" or hiring a professional "crisis manager." **Crisis shouldn't be managed; it should be solved.** The people managers most often choose for their "crisis management" are people who LOVE crisis. Indeed, they often take actions to shut down communications, create a reactive PR mode, and perpetuate the crisis.

If you MUST create a "crisis management team," try to fill it with people who HATE crisis, people who can't wait to get back to normalcy.

Take control of the ball. The simple rule we've learned through many bruising experiences in politics and business is that PR gets very stupid once it moves to the defensive.

Good football teams provide an example of a much better way to act. They play a version of defense that is so aggressive that it is basically offensive. They are constantly going for the ball, grabbing for control. This was perfected inside the Bill Clinton White House. His brilliant counsel, Mark Fabiani, created the "MOD Squad," the "Masters of Disaster." And, of course, their chief gave them plenty of opportunity to perfect their trade. The Clinton White House never played defense at all. When the other team seemed to have the ball, they'd steal it away. They'd go on the offensive immediately—not wildly, but with a strategy to gain control of the dialogue. At the first whiff of trouble—and remember, these pros were never able to see most of these crises coming—they would hunker down quickly to develop a core strategy, knowing that time always works against the defense. You've got to get the ball to score; you've got to score to win.

Respond, don't react. Develop a strategy. Execute it aggressively. Often you'll stun your opponents, who assumed they had control of the momentum. In 1998, in the midst of the Monica Lewinsky story, how many journalists and Republicans confidently predicted that Clinton's presidency wouldn't last the first week? They sat back to let events unfold. And Clinton's communications teams took control. We're not endorsing Clinton's character, just his political skill. And, regardless of your opinion of the man, consider adopting his crisis strategy. It was something like Red Adair's strategy for fighting oil well fires, formed in the heat of a hell of a lot of fires.

Speed wins. The only time you can expect to gain control of the dialogue is at the very beginning of the issue, so you must act quickly. And, without reacting, you must respond. In terms of response, NEVER allow misstatements or mistakes about the issues in your case. Correct every inaccuracy immediately, though politely. This is how NBA coaches keep on top of referees' calls throughout the game, just to get a break on that one call later on. Make people aware of the facts. And hold them to them.

Tell the truth. Years ago, the Venezuelan government hired Scott to do a study of effective communications in the new electronic information age. In the end, the finding was ignored and he was fired. But he was right. Here's what he told them: **The most power-ful form of propaganda is the truth.** In this age, what can be known will be known. Every candidate tells the truth, eventually. And, as we've already said, the only time you have any chance of controlling a crisis is at the very beginning, when control of the dialogue and the attitudes of targets is still being contested. As the advice goes, tell the truth. Tell it all. Tell it fast. H. K. McCann, the founder of the advertising giant McCann Erickson, offered a refinement of this advice: "The Truth Well Told." That's the key: Tell the truth and tell it well. Make your story convincing, but base it on fact. Cleaning up after a lie is much tougher than facing the hard truth immediately. If you're the communications manager, be hard on your managers: Make them tell the truth ruthlessly. It is disarming for your foes and enabling for your friends.

Protect friends and family. In a crisis, inside-out communications are more important than ever. When employees run into the execu-tive stonewall, they often shut down or even turn negative them-selves. While the corporation refuses to say anything, the press, their peers in business, their friends, and even their families may be attacking them with rumors or negative facts.
      We have one commanding rule for our clients: If a crisis communications strategy does nothing else, it must protect friends and family. It must arm them with the truth as you know it, with your side of the story. It must help them understand the weak-ness of the attacks against you. It must allow them to defend them-selves and get back to work. Employees, partners, investors, and

your most loyal customers are your first concern in a crisis. Protect them at all costs. Allow them to do what's in their own best interests—defend you capably and credibly. Identify the friendlies among the Big Mouths and arm them for your defense, as well.

We often provide friends and family with a simple credit-card sized set of facts that tell the story. And we often supplement internal communications with communications sent to the homes of these friends.

@ e-Lessons:

- ☐ e-Marketing is everything-marketing: Every aspect of operations and communications must work from the same script.
- ☐ Develop layer after layer of messages. That's the way you build brandwidth. It takes more and more layers every day to power your way through the noise and clutter.
- ☐ Focus your resources for a powerful blast of messaging, not just a sustained distribution of your messages.
- ☐ PR is marketing. Period. This key communications element must follow the marketing and brand strategies:
  - Develop strategy.
  - Create and tell the brand story, the company story, and the CEO's story about the future.
  - Develop a calendar of information events that support the story.
  - Create a Big Mouth list and keep them constantly informed of your story line.
  - Communicate all information inside out.
  - Work from the ground up.
  - Surround your targets with your stories.
  - Get control of the dialogue in crisis, using the truth as your weapon.

8

FORGET EVERYTHING YOU KNOW ABOUT MASS MARKETING—IT'S OVER

It's like that moment in Steven Spielberg's *Close Encounters of the Third Kind*: A dark and gloomy sky begins to boil with storm clouds. It gathers on the horizon and rapidly spreads over you. There is rolling, rumbling thunder with accompanying flashes of lightning. Now the whole tableau begins to stir, turning slowly around a kind of whirlpool at the center. The rumble and flashing and the John Williams score reach a crescendo. A glow in the middle of all this is growing brighter. And now it's visible. Music up! It fills the screen: the mother ship.

That's the way people have seen the Internet. The Net is HUGE. It's GLOBAL. It's HUMONGOUS. Imagine being able to reach every computer in the world at the same instant. Rumble. Flash. Music up! Like William Shatner says, "This thing is really, really BIG!"

THINK SMALL

But to understand e-marketing and how to build brandwidth on the Net, remember this: the Internet is not about big; it's about small. The Net isn't about covering the globe; it's about reaching the individual. It isn't about everybody; it's about you. **It's about marketing to the market of one.** On the Net you can build brandwidth one consumer at a time. That's the most effective way to do it. That's why when people ask Jeff Bezos what business Amazon.com is in, he answers with their mission statement: "We want to be the number one customer-centric company in the universe."

If you're going to be successful online, you've got to understand the basics of one-to-one marketing. You've got to understand customization, which means you've got to forget everything you know about mass marketing.

To be customercentric these days means to customize to the individual. It means understanding the different segments of the population for whom your product or service has appeal and designing the product around them, designing your marketing around them, or both. **The rule that applies offline and online is simple: never look for efficiency over effectiveness.** Do whatever it takes to remain relevant and different to your core customers.

In many big packaged-goods companies, you haven't made your bones as a brand manager unless you've done national marketing. The idea of going back to market to niche or regional groups seems like a career about-face. On the Net, it's the opposite: If you're going mass, you're the schmuck. The coolness is in nailing smaller groups, and the smaller the better.

THE RISE OF **BIG**

What's good enough for everybody else isn't good enough for you, is it? That's not the way your parents felt in the 1950s, the age of conformity and the dawn of the age of mass marketing. Huge businesses were founded on the standardization of tastes. Holiday Inns and McDonald's, for instance, along with most of the other service and packaged-goods companies, were established on the guarantee that the drab little room you get in Toledo is the same as the one in Tuscaloosa or Tucson.

Television had also taken hold in the land. The three broadcast networks held a monopoly on television and taste-making. Americans were all laughing in unison at the same jokes on *I Love Lucy* and Milton Berle's *Texaco Star Theater*. There was one half hour of network news, delivered by a somber Chet Huntley and David Brinkley or Walter Cronkite, and no more than three news sources a day—the morning newspaper, the network news at 7:00 P.M., and the local news at 11:00 P.M., telling you it was safe to go to bed.

Mass marketing meant one message designed for ALL audiences and the dumbing down of communications to the lowest common denominator in that huge market. Remember Mr. Whipple, Madge the manicurist, and "Ring around the collar!"? If you're over forty, of course you do. Over the years, mass marketing also meant valuing down the product to the most common tastes. That's what mass marketing and its complementary manufacturing philosophy of optimization were all about.

The 1970s were the very top of the roller-coaster ride for optimization and mass marketing. They were absolutely on top of the world, just before they would begin to experience the screaming freefall, like Leonardo DiCaprio shouted before slamming into the iceberg. "I'm king of the world!"

Optimization and mass marketing were the particular philosophy of BIG, BIG, BIG CORPORATIONS. Those were the days of the conglomerate organizations that had no single core competence—except maybe corporate appetite—and amassed a portfolio of basically unrelated businesses, the days when Harold Geneen, the CEO of one of the biggest conglomerates, ITT, reportedly had helpers to carry nine full briefcases for him everywhere. These were "bigness leaders"—corporations that tend to measure their success in volume, are highly bureaucratic, and are formal and heritage-driven. The bigness leaders hated change, because they were doing very well, thank you, based on the status quo. The last thing they wanted was to shake up the "quo" and maybe affect their "status." Our corporate finance systems helped insulate these BIG GUYS. Only highly rated blue chip corporations could issue corporate bonds or raise money through the old-line, "white shoe" brokerages. The big got bigger. And as they grew, they used mass marketing to make their manufacturing processes efficient, to optimize their factory capacities, to push stuff off the loading dock of the factory. **The driving force of mass marketing strategies in those days was distribution—mass distribution.** Stamp it out, shrink-wrap it, and deliver it all over the country, then stack 'em high and price 'em low. So it was also the disassembly of quality and value as core brand components. "Everybody's got one," which would be a suicidal positioning in most markets today, was a very attractive claim back then. Mass had class. Bigness leaders were companies like the Big Three auto makers, heavy manufacturing, banking, and the utility monopolists. Bigness without innovation.

In the early 1980s cracks were beginning to show in optimization as a manufacturing philosophy and mass marketing as the dominant selling process. Companies like Apple and Microsoft, started by "a couple of kids in a garage," baby boomers, were the forerunners of the information economy that would end the incumbent advantages of bigness. They were "change leaders": much less bureaucratic, more mobile and flexible, and driven by the future rather than by heritage. Change leaders love change, because it means opportunity. They are insurgents by their station in the market, but also by nature (Microsoft and Apple both retain that insurgent culture after many years of success—this is how they survived success, in Apple's case just barely and only after bringing back their inspirational change leader, Steve Jobs). Change leaders also began to infiltrate the financial markets, producing revolutionaries like Mike Milken.

People overvalue what they know and undervalue what the benefit of progress will be. So it went for the auto industry. Obsolete yourself, or somebody will do it for you.

To their credit, the Big Three and many other bigness leaders eventually wised up—but not until several hundred thousand American manufacturing jobs had been lost. This time was also the beginning of the end of the stranglehold the three television broadcast networks had on American consumers, as cable television began to tunnel its way across the country. This increase in viewing choices increased the choices in the marketplace, as well. Insurgent marketers like Pepsi, Avis, and Burger King began to establish their brand meanings on the foundation of choice and change, appealing to generational attitudes. It was a perfect time for the insurgent in politics and marketing: Choice and change were powerful themes with boomers and Gen Xers. And they spread to the geezers, as well.

NO INCUMBENT IS SAFE

Stick a fork in it—it's done. Mass marketing is over. Since the information revolution has swept the world economy and changed literally everything in its path, optimization is essentially over, too. Yeah, some companies still hope to get away with limiting consumer choice as a way of making manufacturing more efficient. But with greatly increasing choices on every shelf and the vigorous communication of all those choices on a growing set of media channels, consumers don't buy the idea of "one size fits all." They know if they look a little harder at the market they'll find that "one size that fits just me."

It's a very tough world for incumbents in the marketplace or in politics. And the insurgent culture—promising choice and change—is what even market leaders must adopt to be able to sustain success.

That's because customization rules. People expect more choices and more personal choices. So, today, Holiday Inn is offering three or four different kinds of hotel rooms under different brands (but still way behind the curve of customization, we believe). The folks at Bass (Holiday Inn's adoptive British parent) would be happy, indeed, if Crowne Plaza were never associated with Holiday Inn at all.

And McDonald's recently announced a "Back to the Future" concept called "Made for You": They're going to cook every burger to order; it won't be sitting there under a heat lamp drying out before you get there. McDonald's is a remarkable operations-focused company. They had gotten the standardization thing down to an art and science, a guarantee of the equality of experience from McDonald's to McDonald's all across the land. But McDonald's is also a smart company, so they made changes in the direction the markets are changing. And by 1998, they were finding that close to 50% of the orders placed at the counter or in the drive-thru lane were custom orders: "Give me a Big Mac, but hold the cheese!" "I'll have a double-cheeseburger with extra ketchup." "Can I get bacon on that grilled chicken sandwich?"

This dramatic new advance for McDonald's is just the application of a basic business principle. It's called "Give Consumers What They Want." Ever heard that one before?

The independent, even ornery, nature of today's consumer means you have to create value in different ways from the past and develop a manufacturing and distribution model that will accommodate to that new value system. True, you can't optimize manufacturing plant capacity as easily, but what's the goal—more efficient plants or more sales?

High value often rests with small groups of aficionados of a particular product or service category. The Internet allows you to—no, it demands that you—aggregate geographically diverse people with common interests. So something like Over40.com or LonelyPeople.com or Luxury.com or maybe Diabetics.com or even doggydo.com (yes, dog crap that you can send to your favorite enemy) can find a market effectively and efficiently. Speaking to people with common interests and values means you can speak to groups more personally, as well. Some call this mass customization—really, it's a matter of connection. Like they say, "There's one in every crowd." And the Internet allows you to reach that very one in every crowd. It's the ultimate in choice and personalization: the market of one. **Making, strengthening, and sustaining the connection to target consumers—that's what building brandwidth is all about.**

TALK TALK

All of marketing is a conversation. At its most rudimentary, the conversation is pretty crude—just a consumer's response to the most basic marketing messages: "Hey, you—ALL of you! Buy these socks!"

"No way, Jose!"

But successful marketers have always managed to extend that conversation and personalize it through market research.

"What kind and brand of socks do you usually buy?"

"Do you always buy the same brand? Why?"

"Where do you usually buy them? And why there?"

"What's your greatest gripe about the socks you usually buy? What do you really like about them?"

"What would be the perfect pair of socks for you?"

So the information gets richer, literally more valuable to you. It will inform you of what people are willing to buy long before a stocker puts it on a shelf at Wal-Mart. It will inform your product development process, manufacture, distribution, sales, and marketing.

If you ask Steve Ballmer, the supersalesman at Microsoft, he'll claim all of their market success is based on "super good products," but seldom has a more customer-oriented development and manufacturing process existed. Microsoft's "super good products" come out of their Usability Labs, where they study the way consumers do just about everything they do at home and work and then try to think of ways software can make it better. Microsoft's been criticized in the past for the quality of their initial product introductions, but they operate under the philosophy that "The product is never finished." So they keep improving every product, as long as it exists, using the "conversations" with consumers from the Usability Labs as the foundation for improvement.

The Internet perfects information-based marketing. It perfects the marketing dialogue, allowing the conversation with the customer to be ongoing and constantly improving. Good e-marketers are like brilliant conversationalists. They listen as well as they talk (most marketers are technologically and attitudinally hard of hearing). They keep using what they hear in that discussion to tailor what they say next in the conversation. This is how the Net allows customization. It's wonderful to watch a nine-year-old building a customized skateboard (take a look at sk8shop.com for a great example), selecting board design and size, surface materials, trucks, wheels, and other components, making smart, informed choices all along the way based on the constant dialogue he's having with the Net merchant. It's a conversation that would be inhibited in the BAM (bricks-and-mortar) retail situation, because of the intimidation of an adult salesperson talking to the child.

The smartest marketers on the Net know what most good retailers know: The longer you can keep customers engaged in a conversation, the more you're likely to be able to sell them. In every Net category there is a crowd of competitors. Consumers in every category will visit several of them on a fairly constant basis. Winning, becoming a "market taker," is a matter of winning one more visit and by winning one more minute for the visits you get, then another, then another. **This is what "stickiness" is all about—it's about sticking around. Stickiness can last a long, long time, even in dog years.** Consider Tide laundry detergent. Every year or so, there's a sunburst on the package announcing "TOTALLY NEW NEW NEW" and the addition of blue dots or green dots. All of the changes are product driven and focused on the same target audience, who've moved past Tide on a constant conveyor belt for over fifty years. Product changes lose credibility after people see them over and over. The lesson from Tide is that you build brandwidth any way you have to, laying on more and more and more relevance.

E-CONSUMERS HAVE CHANGED THE RULES

If the Internet's best e-merchants perfect customization, they also condition e-consumers to expect it from ALL merchants. This may be the key effect of e-marketing on BAM marketing so far. It's changing e-consumers, who are changing ALL consumers. That means it's changing the rules of the game for ALL marketers. People are simply learning to expect more. They expect more choices and more personal options. They expect special treatment. They expect to be recognized for their value to the seller. And the contrast between those who give customized service on the Net and elsewhere and those who can't or won't becomes even more distinct.

Even customization can become a commodity. Mileage rewards were differentiated and seemed to be focused on the most important consumers—but for only a short time. Notice how many companies are moving from reward to recognition today. Nobody does a better job than Hertz, with its Platinum service. It's light on the reward side, but very heavy on the recognition side.

Airlines started the mileage reward promotional tactic, but they have been slow to move to recognition. Yet how hard is it to recognize a full-fare business flyer? Almost every other business that awards mileage benefits has done a better job in this transition to recognition than the pioneers of the program have.

This may help account for the widening gulf between most airlines (Southwest and Midwest Express are the unique exceptions) and their frequent business flyer passengers (a high percentage of whom are e-consumers). These airline customers know their value and are increasingly demanding some recognition of it by the big airlines. However, the airlines forget these key passengers are business people and treat them a lot more like a first-time flyer with a backpack.

Frequent business flyers are most often full-fare passengers, since they book at the last minute. A relatively high proportion of these passengers purchase business or first-class tickets, as well. It's a simple fact: In the airline business, you need these passengers to make your nut. It's about Parado's curve, the tendency in any market for a minority of consumers to dominate consumption, sometimes called "the 20/80 rule," meaning 20% of consumers in a market account for 80% of consumption or revenues.

One major airline has a ratio of 3/60—just 3% of its passengers account for 60% of its revenues. But this same airline, like virtually all the others, operates on a philosophy called "yield management." Yield management tries to make sure every seat on an airliner is filled with a paying butt. This strategy considers it sinful if an empty seat flies to Los Angeles. And the airlines have developed software to match promotional offers to those empty seats. You'll see the head-line "$99.00 to Los Angeles," followed by the mouse print: "Certain restrictions apply." The main restriction is that they're only selling the normally empty seats.

Priceline.com developed even more sophisticated software, auc-tioning to consumers the inventory that airlines released to them, seats they didn't expect to fill even at a normal discount. And lastminutetravel.com picks up the very last of the inventory the air-lines will release, having given up on them as hopelessly unmarket-able. These smart guys, led by David Miranda, started as a basic travel agency with a focus on airline tickets and sea cruises, but they zigged and zagged when the market landscape was redefined first by Priceline and then by Expedia.com, Cheaptickets.com, Lowestfare.com, and Evencheapertix.com. David and his people figured the air-lines had to dispose of inventory that was on the very moment of spoilage. "Let's be a marketplace for the most recently released inventory of anything and everything in travel." They had to rethink, reinvent, and move quickly, but they made a success of it.

Now the Assistant to the Assistant Vice President of Yield Man-agement at virtually every major airline has made a momentous suggestion: Once they learned how to sell all the seats on a plane and the information economy provided more flyers, this genius rec-ommended, "Let's put in more seats!" As the average American has gotten a lot heavier and a little taller, the seats and the spaces between them have gotten smaller to accommodate the additional seats that the genius in charge of yield management decided to stuff into the plane.

So these have been good times for airline revenues and lousy times for frequent business flyers. There are more people on the plane, more people crowding the gate, more people tramping through the airports. There are fewer upgrades and fewer opportunities to redeem the miles and miles and miles we are logging on the cramped planes. It makes no sense. They keep making it worse for their best, most profitable customers. Yes, many airlines are insulated by their hub and spoke monopolies, but give these frequent business flyers the chance and they'll bolt. They'll also resist price increases, even if they can't resist "coming back more often to buy more"—that's a function of their booming business, not their satisfaction with the airlines' service, quality, and value. Rob Smith, the top expert on customer relationship management, notes that these airlines create "loyalist terrorists" among their frequent business flyers—customers by force who do nothing but spread negative word-of-mouth advertising. American Airlines found that just one of these loyalist terrorists will infect more than a dozen peers after he or she has had a negative experience on an airliner. And who ever has a really positive one these days?

The airlines are the most clueless businesses about the customer relationship we've ever seen. And they won't be immune from change forever. e-Consumers love a value, but the "price 'em low, stack 'em high" proposition of the traditional discount store has trouble competing in this new environment. As a business flyer, you have to maintain a positive and optimistic attitude. American and United have redefined coach by offering more space (for a higher price, of course, but frequent business flyers are quite willing to pay it). Even at a premium, frequent business flyers think of this advance as designed "just for me."

With the contagion of choices in every market, e-consumers want guidance and navigation through the maze. Internet services like Deja.com (one of our clients, the "buyer's portal") and CNET are designed to provide just that. In other words, you don't have to shop alone. (Try to find a helpful salesperson in the average discount store, or try finding one with an IQ higher than a tube sock.)

And now any shopper can be a smart shopper. After you've been to AutoTrader.com or AutoByTel.com, you're pretty much immune to the average used car salesman. The new car services, even those of the Big Three, are certainly changing the dynamics in the showroom. "Wait here just a minute, I'm going to go ask my manager if I can do a little better on that trade-in" is being replaced by the consumer coming in with a printout: "This is what CarPrices.com says I should be paying."

If you're standing behind a counter at a retailer (department store, fast food joint, brokerage, car dealer, whatever), you'd better be ready to carry on the kind of marketing conversation that's a part of e-tailing, or you're likely to lose the customer. The e-marketing dialogue is central to selling on the Net. Use it or lose. It's increasingly important off the Net, too. That schlub on the other side of the counter is a whole different animal today. Try telling her, "You can't get it that way." Adios.

CREATING "CUSTOMERIZATION"

Customization should be called "customerization," because it's focused on improving and extending the customer relationship and the e-consumer relationship. Remember, usage builds loyalty; it builds brandwidth. So anything you can do to improve and increase usage and increase the velocity of repeat purchase is important. All this can happen in the e-tail dialogue. The better you know the customer, the better you can make the usage experience, and the more opportunity you have to meet the customer's needs (developing relevance) and distinguish yourself from the competition (developing differentiation). **Relevant differentiation is what creates value in any marketplace; it's what creates ROI more certainly than anything else you can do.**

The definition of marketing is simple enough, right? Get more people to come back more often to buy more and be willing to pay more. Never lose sight of that, even for a minute! And you'll do that best concentrating primarily on your current customers.

Customerization is what others call "customer relationship management." The idea is to maximize the lifetime value of your customer's relationship with your company and brands. This is the antidote for the mass marketing churn. Most mass marketers traditionally ignored the customers—they were essentially blind to them. They didn't recognize the value of any one customer, only of ALL of them. When the customer returned more often to buy more, the mass marketers had no way of knowing it or rewarding it. The mass marketer would sell a few million people a box of Sudzo, then have to go out and sell the next box to them all over again, remarketing over and over again. Remarketing is highly inefficient and very, very expensive.

Customerization recognizes the efficiency of getting repeat purchase versus getting the initial sale. **Customerized marketing, or customer relationship management, focuses on the pragmatic issue of building share of customer over share of market.** There's a lot less wind resistance in asking your current customer for a little more usage of the product or service, or for one more purchase, than in trying to seek out a new customer or open up a new market. Almost no brand has 100% loyalty of its customers. For instance, the vast majority of Coke drinkers also drink Pepsi (and other soft drinks). The vast majority of Pepsi drinkers also drink Coke. **Winning share of customer means winning one more drinking occasion over the competition.**

- ☐ You build share of market on share of customer.
- ☐ You build it one usage occasion at a time, not just one consumer at a time.
- ☐ And, as we've said again and again, as you build brand usage, you build brand loyalty.

The way to build share of customer is to make sure the product, package, price, merchandising, promotion, user support, PR, and advertising meet a customer's needs better, by customizing all of those communications links to the needs of the individual as much as possible. The more personal the communications, the more likely they are to motivate personal decisions. So you want to drill them down to the smallest possible market: The Net lets you do so—one customer at a time. The Net maximizes the return on customerization because it allows you to connect the smallest, most geographically diverse interest groups effectively and efficiently. It can aggregate the "market of one."

Mass marketing is a pretty inefficient way to convince current customers to do anything. What's the chance that millions of people share the same needs, wants, and tastes? These days, less than zero. Only the biggest customer franchises, like Budweiser or Coke, can hope to stimulate mass purchase with that broad an effort.

HOW THE NET SAVED ADVERTISING

Just when TV advertising was becoming an exorbitantly expensive irrelevancy, the Net came along and saved its ass. Amazing.

Over the past decade, network TV advertising had been losing relevance among big advertisers, and the networks were losing audience to cable and other alternatives at the level of a major hemorrhage. Although a Budweiser or Coke can hope to use advertising to stir mass purchase, it's still pretty tough to recommend broadcast TV advertising as a $600 million marketing tool to a big national brand.

In the marketing cacophony of the age, consumers are making choices closer and closer to the point of purchase. And that's where you want to aim your marketing bucks. Consumers are not marching to the store whistling the jingle of their favorite brands any more. Take a look at your own shopping list: Chances are it doesn't say, "Coca-Cola and Sprite, Tide, Crest, Scott tissue." More likely, it's "Soda, detergent, toothpaste, toilet paper." The brand will be decided when you get to the store, in fact, when you get to the shelf. You have no doubt the big brands will be there. And you may wait to be moved by a niche brand or new choice or new promotion on the shelf next to your usual brand. There's no brandwidth to products that are selling on the basis of "okay product/great price."

Distribution and slotting, packaging, pricing, merchandising, and promotion in the store can be a lot more effective than TV advertising in moving the customer's hand that four or five inches from one brand to another, once he gets to that shelf.

These in-store and grassroots tactics are very hard working, but TV advertising is pretty lazy marketing. Big marketing clients have been pushing for new, more productive approaches as alternatives to broadcast TV, but the ad industry has resisted the push.

Remember, the big ad agencies, with their sky-high operating costs, really aren't making money unless they are producing or placing network TV advertising. PR agencies aren't making money unless they're producing press release tonnage. Broadcast TV has been ad agencies' answer to every marketing problem. Bales of press releases have been the PR agencies' panacea. Another T-shirt and coffee cup with your name on it have been the standard marketing promotions.

The ad agencies aren't alone in their push for mass marketing tactics over other, more focused tactics. Most brand managers working for anything from a startup to the bluest of chips don't feel they're really in marketing unless they're in television advertising, big national PR campaigns, and huge promotional efforts. You mean you don't have a blimp?!

If you're the brand manager, would you rather organize an in-store promotion for your new cereal in Akron and Altoona, or fly first-class to Fiji to stay in a luxury hotel with a bunch of hip ad people to shoot a commercial for it with Joe Pytka? Or how about going to the Daytona 500 to feast on hors d'oeuvres and cold Bud surrounded by NASCAR heroes and honeys, watching to see how your sticker looks on the back bumper of the car. Come on. Tell the truth.

Still, clients have been demanding results more and more often and tactical marketing companies have had to develop the means to deliver them. Clients have also been turning the thumb screws on agency commissions and fees. So things looked pretty glum for the industry . . .

Until the Net came along and brought thousands of prospective new clients.

We've looked at the phenomenon of Web startups doing TV advertising for all the wrong reasons and in all the wrong ways. But the fact is mass communication can make sense for many, many Net companies. The Web is just extending past its early adopter stage: Usage is growing quickly, but still is controlled by a minority of the population on both the consumer and business side. Still, virtually everybody is going to the Net. Draw a pyramid on a piece of scrap paper. At the top, maybe a third of the way down, draw a horizontal line. Above that are people and companies who are already using the Net. Below that are people and companies who WILL be using the Net. At the base of the pyramid is EVERYBODY.

Broad communications can make sense. On the consumer side, usage will grow rapidly with the convergence of traditional television and Internet information services. On the business side, there's almost no company that will not be on the Net over the next four to five years, no matter the size or industry. People will buy everything from heavy machinery to hand towels, from raw materials to office supplies, over the Net. The aggregation of sellers will give buyers more choice. The aggregation of buyers will open new markets for sellers. B2B (business-to-business) e-commerce will shortly account for 10% of all business purchases, on its way toward 80% or 90% eventually.

The Internet pipeline will flow like a gusher over time. Right now, moving businesses and consumers into it faster is a key business priority for all Net firms and their investors; this will speed up their eventual payday. The PC revolution was agonizingly slow in its penetration. The Internet revolution has to go faster to create the markets that will justify the "excessive exuberance" in Net companies' shares that Alan Greenspan drones on about.

Almost all people and certainly all business people must be made aware of new brands, what these brands stand for, why they should care about them, what makes them different from other brands, and what makes them worth the price they charge. In other words, brandwidth must be developed and continually widened with an ever-expanding group of Web consumers and Web companies.

Given the enormity of the audience, this is a strong case for mass media to communicate marketing messages—probably the strongest case since mass marketing and mass media came to power in the 1940s and 1950s. But, of course, mass media and mass ANYTHING will have to be rethought. It will still have to be based on that very inconvenient process called "strategy." On political business in Africa a long time ago, Scott asked the local contact about a particularly curious event.

"What's the reason for it?" we asked.

"Oh, you Americans will never understand African politics. You assume there must be a reason for things."

We still believe that. There MUST be a reason.

Communicating to the huge potential Net audience makes sense. It sometimes also makes sense to communicate through broad-reach media to the current, smaller audiences of Web consumers, e-businesses and Web investors, analysts, and other decision and value shapers. This is "broadcasting narrow news," not "narrowcasting." Sometimes it's perfectly sensible to use a mass medium to reach a smaller audience.

Look at the strategy at work at Turner's cable properties (what are they called now? Time/Warner/Steve/Ross/Ted/AOL?). Steve Heuer, Turner's chief architect and president, has used broad media to reach a narrow audience on CNN, CNNfn, CNNSI, TBS, TNT, Turner South, and Cartoon Network. The formula is to target the audience and adjust the content. It's a very un-TV idea, but it works.

The landgrab mentality on the Net and elsewhere is not hysteria—it's for real. And it may justify overspending to build brandwidth now for the payoff later. Your three favorite Web sites are now flanked by two or three more just like them. Which will survive and thrive? There will be only two or three winners at the top of any category. Which will be eaten by one of the brands that will survive? Which will be forced into the niche/specialized bottom of the market? Which will somehow e-vaporate—the statistics on new business failures still run at about the traditional 80% rate. A startup, on the Net or anywhere else, has about the same chances of survival as the first troops hitting the beaches of Normandy on D-Day.

If your company is going to be a winner, it's going to have to build brandwidth right now with those most important audiences listed above. You must start to win right now if you want to win BIG in three or four years. So your marketing has to mature a lot faster than marketing for traditional BAM companies. e-Marketers hit puberty at about three months old.

Competing now for brandwidth a few years from now doesn't mean just blasting out "awareness advertising" on mass media. **Awareness that's not connected to brand meaning and differentiation quickly fades**—and we've seen plenty of examples of foundering Web ideas already in the short history of the medium. It's crucial to enrich the awareness of audiences already familiar with the Net and to activate their powerful effect as word-of-mouth advertising media in themselves. This means building a solid base for further growth. And that can't be done simply by making them more aware of the brand—they must be made more aware of what the brand means to them personally. So your mass messages will have to encourage mass usage; if you don't engage usage, brand awareness is meaningless. **Even mass messages must be made as personal and customized as possible. They must have their effect one consumer at a time.**

As we've said, the concept of inevitability is very strong right now. At this stage of the Internet's development and given its rapid growth among Web consumers and businesses, there's great power in communicating convincingly, "This is the way it's going to be" and "We'll be there, when you get there."

Many Net firms have done this effectively, too—we've cited the example of Priceline.com ("I'm tellin' ya, this is gonna be BIG!!"). To both current and potential Net users in B2C (business to consumer) and B2B, the message "Why would you [shop, buy, sell, search, etc.] any other way?" is very powerful. These early users want to be using the best the Web has to offer.

Get used to it. **MASS MARKETING IS OVER. WHAT'S GOING TO REPLACE MASS MARKETING IS WHAT YOU MIGHT CALL "*MAS* MARKETING" FROM THE SPANISH WORD FOR "MORE" MARKETING.** "Mas marketing" is going to take more work, more drilling down to consumers' individual wants and needs, more customized messaging to them. The job just keeps getting tougher and tougher. But the rewards for e-ffective marketing just keep getting better and better. The Net does searches in two directions: It finds valuable information, products, and services for Web consumers and business, and it also finds valuable customers for e-marketers. What a deal.

e-Lessons:

- To learn e-marketing, you might have to unlearn the mass marketing principles that have dominated most of big brand marketing for almost half a century.
- The Net is not about mass marketing, but about *mas* marketing, doing more with each individual customer, using customization to build brandwidth with him or her. To do this, you've got to establish an active consumer dialogue, an ongoing conversation in which you make it worth consumers' while to help you customize to their needs and desires.
- Not all of the tactics of mass marketing are dead—mass broadcast is working to help build Internet brands with current and future users among consumers and businesses. Just remember that awareness isn't enough: You've got to create relevance and differentiation; you've got to define the brand and explain why it's going to be important to its users.
- In e-marketing, communicate to the smallest groups of people you possibly can, and you'll be able to speak most personally to them. That's the likeliest way to build real value.

9

TO BUILD BRANDWIDTH, BUILD ON THE CONCEPTS OF E-MERCHANTING

e-Marketing seems to have encouraged everybody to try to circumvent the basics. "This is a new, new thing. We've got to make its marketing new, New, NEW!"

But the Net itself is not so much new, new, new as it is a new take on the basics. Marketing, no matter how new its development, must achieve an age-old result. It must sell. It's done that for literally thousands of years, following principles that predate mass marketing, advertising, and modern PR. e-Marketing is based on the fundamentals of the merchant-consumer relationship, what we call "e-merchanting." These principles have been improved over time, but never changed. And they drive the newest iteration of marketing, building brandwidth, because the basic assumption of e-marketing is selling one customer at a time. **Yes, this implies a significant shift in the nature of marketing from the highly impersonal, highly inefficient methods of mass marketing to the highly personal, efficient methods of customized marketing.**

THE RETURN OF THE MERCHANT

The end of mass marketing signals the beginning of the emergence (or reemergence after a sixty-year coma) of personalized merchanting, the personalized approach that our forefathers and foremothers enjoyed as a basic tenet of doing business. Merchanting preceded mass marketing and will survive it, because customization will always win out over optimization, as long as it is made a choice in the marketplace.

The concept of merchanting existed long ago because it had to. (After all, social and economic imperatives influence the marketplace more than anything else, right?) **At the time, our lives were limited by geography and primitive transportation to our own communities—yet competition always existed.** Kindly old Fred, who owned the vegetable stand, was nice to you because he knew that if he wasn't, you might frequent kindly old Mario's vegetable stand down the street. Fred remembered—and often kept records to keep his memory honest—what kind of onions you liked, how many potatoes you bought, and how often you bought them in order to provide an ease of transaction called convenience, or personal service.

Fred's business depended on your satisfaction and repeat business. After all, he had to keep on feeding his kids every day. He wanted you to spend a few more minutes over the eggplant and carrots and iceberg lettuce. So he'd look for ways to engage you in conversation. Idle chitchat wouldn't get him very far. You were focused on dinner, not the weather or the Red Sox. It'd be better to talk about what you're thinking about, which is vegetables and dinner. If he could give you helpful information about vegetables or how to prepare them, he'd be a lot likelier to hold you there and to get you to buy more, come back more often, and maybe even pay more for special items or for his knowledge about ordinary items. (Doing all that, he'd be a marketing ace in any age.) So this may sound very familiar.

His goal then was the same as the goal of Safeway or Wal-Mart today. Or AskJeeves.com, or Amazon.com, or any dot.com that understands the value of repeat business. Get them and keep them.

The interactive capability of the Internet provides the potential for a similar kind of personalization of the selling process, as well as the opportunities for tracking customer preferences and offering real-time responses.

In theory, all marketing is a dialogue, right? In the marketplace of a hundred years ago, that dialogue was characterized by haggling. The seller communicated; the buyer responded; the seller responded. The consumer method of "walking away three times" is thousands of years old and still practiced today on Priceline.com, the reverse auction, and eBay, the true auction. The idea for both of them is to sell the most inventory—much better to sell stuff to those who are willing to buy it than to have it sitting in a warehouse. The concept is the same as B2B (business-to-business) marketplaces—matching buyers and sellers. And this is what all marketplaces have been doing for a few thousand years.

The Internet allows you to know what's happening as it's happening. It makes it possible for a marketer in Battle Creek, Michigan, to know more about customers in Birmingham, Alabama, or Bangor, Maine, and to know it instantly to translate it faster to the shelf at their local market. Or, anyway, it SHOULD. We are astounded at the slow response times of BAMs (bricks-and-mortars) to the opportunity of the Net. There is one hell of a lot of fear and loathing out there. We noted earlier that most BAMs have established task forces to plan their move to the Internet (most often, this plan consists of copying down the phone number of Ariba), and these task forces are being led by the CEO in almost half the cases. Often, the CEO's leadership toward the Net is about as confident as a kid's confidence heading into the dentist's chair. Their B2B strategies often show this tentativeness—maybe that's why so many are off to such a slow start.

Empowered with this instant, Web-enabled knowledge, you can then sell more of what's selling: We call it "momentum marketing." By marketing what's selling, you tell consumers that you understand and anticipate their needs. This isn't magic; it's common sense. And common sense will put a lot of charlatan gurus out of business. Won't that be a shame?

In the current economic model, mass retailers have a financial need to sell you what THEY'RE buying, because they have warehouses full of stuff they bought (bets they made months ago and that often were fixed by the manufacturers' paying slotting, marketing, and promotional allowances to influence the retailers' buying decisions). This is a concept called "buying to buy," rather than "buying to sell." You do high fives for good purchasing from the supplier, not good selling to the consumer: "Boy we really squeezed a great deal out of that manufacturer."

And the manufacturer leaves the deal with nothing available to promote the sales of the product. That leaves the retailers with only one option: They bought it cheap and they have to sell it cheap. Make that a low five instead of a high five. Essentially, the manufacturers are paying the retailers to sell you the stuff in the warehouses. "It's December 26. Let's sell Christmas decorations!"

And people will always be willing to buy on that basis. They just won't be willing to pay.

But e-merchants want to sell you only what you're willing to pay for. (Yes, there are already promotional services on the Net that will reward your buy; Netcentives is a good example. But these services reinforce a buying decision and don't influence it. They encourage repurchase more than purchase.) Push marketing will never beat personalized marketing. Period. Like the direct marketers long before them, e-marketers commit only to the inventory they need, when they need it to meet your needs. And that is always AFTER they sell it to you.

Let's look at an example from the book business. Borders and Barnes & Noble: *markets*. Amazon.com: *merchant*. Borders and Barnes & Noble sell books, but they undoubtedly make a lot of their money *buying* books, that is, getting marketing and promotional allowances from the big publishing houses. So, while they are certainly willing to sell you the book you want to buy, they for SURE want to sell you the book they bought a lot of or essentially got paid by a publisher to sell. That's why you have to navigate through those stacks of books on tables and stacks of books on the floor and stacks of books on books (*The Wines of Portugal, The Gardens of Cardiff, The Doors of Simi Valley*) to get to the book you want to buy.

Amazon.com does business fundamentally differently. They simply ask, "What book do you want to buy?" and get it for you, reasonably inexpensively and reasonably quickly (relative to getting it instantly at a bookstore). Amazon also does an incredibly good job of defining expectations to deliver customer satisfaction: Who'd have thought you'd be perfectly happy to get the book you really want three days from the time you buy it? Amazon asks, and then listens to what you say. That makes them smarter than Borders or Barnes & Noble (who are getting smarter all the time, themselves). You ask questions, you get smart. So they keep asking, after the purchase: "Geez, since you like Tom Clancy, did you get his brand new book?" or "Since you like the new American cuisine, did you get the new cookbook by Monique Barbeau?" The Amazon model is based on those two key questions of the traditional merchant: "What can I do for you?" and "What else can I do for you?"

ORGANIC MARKETING

What Amazon.com does is not just pull marketing—helping consumers do what they want to do—but *organic marketing*—

forming marketing around consumers' needs and wants. As David Risher, senior VP of product development for Amazon said recently, "In the online world, it's difficult to discern what is marketing and what is product development."

That's the whole idea of e-merchanting. Product development means producing and packaging products as if every one is personalized: "Here, Mrs. Smith," says kindly old Fred, the vegetable man. "I've saved these tomatoes for you to make that Greek salad tonight."

These are not just any tomatoes—they're YOUR tomatoes.

Product development must be established out of the consumer dialogue (as Bill Gates has shaped Microsoft's Usability Labs to do). Otherwise, the product misses the market, particularly the newly reinvigorated market of one. You can't count on the limited choice range of mass marketing to protect you. You can't rely on mass marketing's push tactics to help you. You've got to relearn. This is totally new stuff, unless you're over seventy years old.

Organic marketing differs from mass marketing by asking rather than telling. Organic marketing is high touch, enabled by high tech. It's selling what you can sell based on what consumers will buy. By asking smart questions and listening carefully to the answers, you begin to seem very intuitive. You seem to anticipate the buyers' needs. That makes them very happy. And that has made Amazon.com very, very, very successful (at least with investors and, sooner or later, with consumers). Have you gotten e-mail from Amazon.com saying, "We checked what you bought last and thought you'd be interested in this"? These people are true e-merchants.

Organic marketing eliminates the curse of dead merchandise. The concept of dead merchandise was developed by the legendary Toshifumi Suzuki, the marketing genius of Ito Yokado, Japan's retail food chain. He believed that any merchandise that didn't turn frequently, merchandise that was passed up by consumers on two or three store visits, was essentially dead merchandise. It had a consumer curse on it. And that curse infected the products around it . . . in fact, the whole store. Suzuki's premise (proven in great success) was that inventory should be totally revised on a weekly basis. It was an imperfect database: He asked his sales people to look at the customer and try to record information about them from memory. But it was a lot better than nothing. It allowed them to figure out who was buying and what to sell them. After 7-Eleven managed itself into bankruptcy in the U.S., 7-Eleven Japan bought the chain. Actually all the Japanese wanted to purchase were the 7-Eleven stores in Hawaii. They were concerned that the poor management of these stores would hurt their brand image with Japanese tourists. It turned out that for the price of Hawaii and California, they could get the whole deal.

The also legendary retailer Mickey Drexler of Gap, Inc. revolutionized clothes retailing by totally reinventing the pace of remerchandising his Gap stores. The accepted pace of his department store competitors was methodical and slow ("Back to School," "Happy Holidays," "Swing into Spring"), so Drexler developed a weekly change of merchandise within his Gap stores. He measured this pace on the attention span of his best customers, not his occasional customer. He generated sales at the core of this franchise. And the heat at the core erupted into widespread sales growth. He now runs circles around the competition. He's done so by making a science of watching his customers more closely and reacting faster than any of his competitors and, particularly, his department store sources of business (Mickey sees them not as competition but as feeder opportunity). Gap doesn't try to establish fashion trends, or even approach the cutting edge (don't tell this to Mickey, or you'll get an argument—nevertheless it's true). What they do is follow their customers so closely that it seems their fashion is part of their customers' lives, so that it seems the brand is intuitive about their wants and needs.

When you market what's selling, you convince your customers you're really on top of things—you sell the most popular stuff (on their terms).

Great merchants have always worked this way, and the best of them still do. The great mass of mass merchandising and mass marketing is a one-sided conversation: The retailers yell into the darkness and hope (if they yell loud enough and often enough) that somebody hears them. That's push marketing.

Ninety percent of the time, nobody responds. According to day-after recall scores, at least 80% of the television audience never even remembers the advertising you ran, much less is motivated by it to go out and buy. Mass marketing calls for loading and reloading the shotgun again and again and blasting away into the darkness. Most of the shot falls to earth harmlessly; in fact, tons and tons of lead fall every day. The only sure winners in this equation are the mass media. They get paid by the ounce.

The lesson for e-marketing is damn simple: Sell what they want to buy. Then focus on selling them some more. This sale should establish the foundation for the next sale. As you're readily aware, the major airlines don't do a very good job of using the transaction as a sales opportunity. Instead, they unsell you with lousy service. How ignorant is that?? Push marketing yells, "Come and get it!" Pull marketing says, "Here's YOUR product."

And nothing activates organic marketing like allowing satisfied consumers to go to work as your most convincing medium of communications. It's a quiet, but profound, revolution.

Mass marketing, push marketing, calls for a high-decibel monologue. In contrast, pull marketing is established on a real and active dialogue, virtually face-to-face. It asks, "What do you want? What can I do especially for you?

And it promises only what it can deliver: "I have what you want" or "I'll get what you want."

This was the promise of the brilliant theme line the ad agency Weiden & Kennedy came up with for Microsoft: "Where do you want to go today?"

It's a line we're not sure their client really understands. Because too often Microsoft and other powerful Internet businesses have fallen into the tired old mass marketing refrain: "I'll tell you where you want to go today." They want to sell features—what THEY can do—not benefits—what YOU can do. As always, Dan Weiden was ahead of his time.

WIth choice so readily available on the Net, force doesn't and can't win. Net consumers want to learn to trust their guides through the Web. Once trust is established (by clearly defining expectations and then overdelivering on them), they actually will appreciate the guide's streamlining their choices, making recommendations based on the dialogue between them. But trust can evaporate when those recommendations are based on deals the portal made for key word placement or exclusive relationships with various other Web providers.

Lately, a shift away from the big, established Net portals toward newer, more open spaces has occurred, as Web users learn their own navigational tricks and learn more about the choice limitations of their original portals. In the information revolution, choice always beats force, eventually. Go long on choice and short on force. What you may be betting is your career.

e-Lessons:

□ Over the past sixty years, the marketplace has gone from personal to impersonal to personal again. If you're going to establish brand relationships with consumers, you need to relate to them not just with product or package or price or merchandising, but with information and interaction. What changed first on the Net is not the way people sell, obviously, but the way they buy. Consumer expectations have changed completely and continue to change. How consumers interact with you and what they expect from you, no matter what business you're in, will be shaped by ALL of their marketing relationships, not just the one they have with you and not just over the Net, but over the counter as well. Most marketing managers think only in terms of category, but in fact all marketing influences all other marketing.

☐ Everybody must learn this e-lesson, because the Internet has created the most dramatic kind of corporate *jiujitsu*. It has allowed startups with few material assets to play even with huge companies, leveraging the advantage of their own understanding of e-marketing and exploiting the momentum of the bigger corporations' tendencies toward outmoded mass marketing against them. Research now shows that all consumers (Net users or not) perceive that a dot.com is simply smarter than an established BAM in the same category. And, as usual, consumer perceptions are right. It's not that traditional businesses are brainless, but that many of them are clueless about the Internet.

☐ The bigger the company, the more likely they are to see the Internet simply as more distribution (they are likely to think "more" rather than "better"). They see it simply as a way to distribute their basic business model and marketing model farther and faster.

☐ Think merchanting, not just marketing. Focus on the relationship, not just the sale. That's the Amazon.com model, and it will work for you, whether you sell beans, Beanie Babies, bolts, or BMWs.

10

BRANDWIDTH IS ALLERGIC TO SAMENESS

In both versions of Disney's *Fantasia* there's a sequence that graphically captures what's happening in every category on the Net (and off the Net, too). It's "The Sorcerer's Apprentice." Mickey Mouse is the apprentice to a great sorcerer, but his job is totally menial, mopping up the sorcerer's castle. He finds the sorcerer's magic wand and magic hat. This is great! He can command the bucket and mop to do the work for him. It's so easy that Mickey falls asleep—and while he sleeps, the magic makes the mops and buckets proliferate, marching to the well for more water, sloshing it over the floor of the castle until Mickey and everything else in there is bobbing around in the flood.

The *Fantasia* nightmare is reality in the marketplace: We're all bobbing around in a sea of sameness. In every category more and more new brands appear, but they appear more and more like one another, all of them related like kissing cousins to the market leader. Starbucks breaks new ground, and fifty more gourmet coffee shops open up, with gourmet coffee brands breeding like bunny rabbits everywhere from Wal-Mart to the mall.

In the early days of the Net, every brand leader in every category was new and unique. Usually the leader WAS the category. Success breeds imitation, of course, and so sameness has arrived on the Net big time. Same looks, same feel, same approach in e-brand after e-brand and e-marketing program after e-marketing program. Every market has a whole lot more "see you," with the same claims being made, than "raise you," with new and different claims. Building brandwidth means building relevant differentiation into everything you say and do. Just look on a supermarket shelf or surf a Net category on eTour. How many brands are truly different?

On a political assignment Scott would love to forget, he was once sent to Khartoum, Sudan, where dust permeates the skin and heat invades your brain. He'd get in the security guy's car, drive out of the hotel parking lot, and immediately hit one of Khartoum's famous "go slow"s, or traffic jams, and be gridlocked for hours. He asked Ali, the security guard, how this could be happening. After all, there were only ten thousand or so automobiles in the entire nation. How could they all end up in the same traffic jam at the same time every day? "It's the herding instinct," he told him.

Marketing suffers from this madness, too. It's called the "sameness instinct." **Everyone knows the importance of developing relevance and differentiation in marketing (that's the surest way to develop return on investment or assets). So why is it that nobody tries very hard to develop meaningful differentiation? Why is the favorite brand positioning in any category "me, too"?**

It's happened on every shelf in the market, and now it's happening on the Internet. But of course. First the categories crowd with competitors, and then the herding instinct takes over.

Sites are appearing on the Net like people jamming onto the A train at rush hour. The Net itself was a novelty less than five years ago. One entrant held each of the new categories of e-commerce, like the first "Sooners" staking out claims in the Oklahoma land rush. But on the Net, staking out a claim guarantees you no sovereignty over the territory. You wake up one morning and find two or three new squatters on your turf. The next day, five or six more. And, maddeningly, they're all walking and talking and dressing and acting just like you.

It's the sameness instinct—the warmth and security of the crowd. And overcrowding in this space is the same as overcrowding in any other ecosystem: eventual famine and death for most of the herd.

THE NEED FOR CAP AND GAP

Geoffrey Moore writes compellingly about the development of the e-conomy in his books *Crossing the Chasm* and *Inside the Tornado.* Recently, he related the importance of breaking away from the herd on the Net. What develops value on the Internet is "cap and gap," meaning the market cap and the gap of differentiation between you and the competitive pack. The company that develops that combination of high cap and high gap wins the value war. In fact, it's been estimated that the difference in value between the number 1 and number 2 competitors in any e-commerce market is a multiple of twenty times in value! The thing to realize is that the high cap is impossible without the high gap. Differentiation creates value. Scarcity creates value: That accounts for the price of diamonds; that accounts for the price you're willing to pay a locksmith late on a bitter winter's evening when you're locked out of your house.

Gratuitous difference won't do the job (like advertising with the nose ring). The difference must be meaningful to consumers; it must be difference on the issues they care about in making purchasing decisions.

REPETITIVELY, REDUNDANTLY REPEATING

The sameness instinct is proof that most business people are followers. Sorry. And we hope you're not one of them. But how else do you explain the vast sea of sameness in every category? Instead of looking at consumers in a marketplace, they tend to look at companies, particularly the market leaders. "I want to be like them!"

And who wouldn't want to be like the rich and powerful market leader? So they try to act and look like them. They copy the product as closely as they can, as long as there's not proprietary technology—and even proprietary technology has a shorter shelf life at a time when a company like Sun Microsystems or Oracle can devote five or ten thousand developers to covering your market offer. They copy the packaging, the customer interface, the merchandising, the marketing, the sponsorships, the stuff and stuff and stuff.

This crowding calls on the true quality of leadership: the commitment to stay ahead of the pack, whatever it takes. The change is prompted by an awareness of competition forming up around your current offer. After all, it's so easy on the Internet to find out exactly what your competitors offer. Although it may be prompted by competition, change at your company must be focused just where it should be—not only on the competition, but on the customers' needs and wants.

The shelf life of strategic differentiation is shorter than ever. You've got to be on the move to be in the lead. It's true, too, that the follower instinct of the increasing competitive crowd usually helps insulate leadership and deaden the sense of challenge to the status quo. **In the end, most of these competitors don't actually expect to replace the market leader—they just want to imitate them and maybe share a little of the wealth.** Look how thick the Yellow Pages are—if they carried only the telephone numbers of companies providing relevant differentiation, they could be sent out on a double-sided Xerox copy. The sameness instinct is not a winning instinct, but a survival instinct. Yet what's happening is just the opposite.

GOOD-BYE MIDDLE MARKET

It isn't just market leaders who suffer in the sameness syndrome that's crowding the Net—think of the poor consumers, having to wade through the market mush.

Will the crowd just keep building and building in every category? That's not the way we see it. Instead, in every market in which we've worked, from book publishing to securities to sneakers to soda pop to software, we see a similar pattern emerging in which the middle market, that ill-defined sea of sameness, is drying up, disappearing.

As clutter has proliferated, consumer behavior has changed the competitive situation in all of the markets we work in or observe. Consumers still look for that one or perhaps two brands at the top of the market that represent a sure thing—sure to be available, acceptable, and affordable virtually anywhere.

Still, as we've said again and again, this is the time of reemerging customization. So consumers also go to specially focused brands that appeal to special needs and wants. Personalization builds brandwidth.

Consumers are bypassing the middle market in every category. The middle players are dying off or getting gobbled up and consolidated into the market leaders' increasing businesses. There will continue to be vitality at the top and bottom of every market, but the middle is no-brand's land.

This consolidation is coming to every business, and it's coming to the Net. Do we really need 19 choices for purchasing a car on the Internet? Look at the number of monkey-see, monkey-do competitors in the travel business. Back in the dark days of the Cold War with the Soviet Union, we saw a sign in a bar that captures our rec-ommendation to the e-companies stuck in that middle tier today: "In case of nuclear attack—loosen belts, ties and shoelaces; remove eye-glasses; bend over with your head between your knees; kiss your ass good-bye."

BREAKING AWAY

Our recommended solution to getting stuck in the middle is the same old thing we always preach: difference, difference, difference. Drive relevant differentiation into everything you do. Start it with the most important communication of brand, the product. Drill differentiation into marketing communications of all kinds. Push differentiation into your customer relationship. Take relevant differentiation down to the micro level.

Once you've done that, then what? Keep changing. The market leader in any category is dedicated to operational excellence. They're obsessed with relevant differentiation (that's how they got to be the leaders).

Most companies work hard to get their market offer right. But we've got bad news—"right" is a moving target. To keep getting it right, you can't sit still; you've got to keep moving. If you look behind you, you'll see a crowd of competitors sneaking up. So you keep looking ahead at the consumer. Your customers will show you the way to meaningful difference: They'll tell you what it will take to meet their needs uniquely. And, thanks to the Net, you don't have to wait until they vote against you with their feet (or finger, in this case); you can know instantly and constantly where you stand rela-tive to the competitive pack. Keep moving ahead, eyes on the road. Avoid the temptation to look in that rear-view mirror. When we consulted to Time, Inc. in the 1980s this was the way the magazine's entire management drove into the future, fixated on *Newsweek* behind them, copying almost everything *Newsweek* did. This not only narrowed the gap between them, but did a job on *Time*'s cap, even then. With the two top competitors in weekly news magazines fixated on each other and virtually ignoring their customers, they destroyed their own category.

BUILDING BARRIERS TO ENTRY

With the sameness that's permeating Net sites and service development and overrunning Net marketing communications, the barriers to entry in any Internet category are getting lower and lower. These days they're more like speed bumps than real barriers.

It's like what happened in the convenience-store business that was dominated early on by 7-Eleven. The business was simple and simply dominated by beer, cigarettes, soda pop, snacks, and other staples of the core market of young, male, blue-collar workers. Those items accounted for the lion's share of revenues in the business: For the sake of convenience, these young guys were willing to pay a heavy markup. It didn't take long for the gas station across the road from the 7-Eleven to catch on to the formula. Take out one service bay and you could put in a cooler, a cigarette rack, some chips, and a cash register—and, bingo, you're a 7-Eleven, too! Southland, 7-Eleven's owner, kept trying to up the ante, offering everything from video rentals to flower sales to gourmet foods. But that didn't change the basic equations of the business. Now everything but local banks are in the convenience-item business. (And a couple of local bankers, reading this, are going, "Hmmmmm . . .")

This is what's happening in every market everywhere, and the Net isn't spared. Like they say, there's somebody in a garage somewhere loading an Internet bullet with the name of your company on it, ready to send you to an early grave. But chances are the bullet will miss you. And they'll take their place right beside you, ready to be a good neighbor in your category, sharing the wealth. So the choice is die fast or die slowly: Sameness drains the value out of any category. It takes the vitality out of once active and growing segments of business.

Still, when we have our initial meetings with Internet companies and ask them, "Who's the competition?", they invariably answer confidently: "Nobody does what we do."

Sure. According to whom? **Once your category begins to be overrun with similar-sounding claims, obfuscating information, and a dizzying array of brands and sites and services, the size of the competitive field explodes in the perceptions of consumers. Those formerly clearly demarcated category divisions come tumbling down.** "Is this a car-buying site or a car buyers' service site? Oh, well . . . whatever."

The early Net pioneers challenged the status quo, helping to define a new and important business evolution. They boldly reconceptualized business processes and reevaluated business markets. They were courageous and adventurous. They had a buccaneer spirit toward change. They played this game with abandon. And they tooled the engines that would change absolutely everything in business, on and off the Net.

Now the settlers are pouring into the fertile land of the Net, believing that gold will jump out of the ground and into their pockets. They're perfectly happy to settle for their own little piece of the status quo—they don't want to change a thing. And therein lies the danger for the pioneers. It's getting mighty crowded out there where the frontier used to be; strip malls and housing developments are popping up all over. Some of those pioneers, who seemed like Paul Bunyan in the old, uncrowded days of the early Web, now are getting lost in a crowd of Elmer Fudds. Indeed, as consumers struggle through the frustration of searching this immense space now, some of them aren't even managing to wade through to the pioneers' sites they used to visit so often. Whole categories are losing their differentiation.

REBUILDING, BRICK BY BRICK

You can't sit still and allow this competitive market free-for-all to develop. The question now is, were you the smart little pig, building a barrier of solid brick? Or are you the one with the sticks that can be scattered by a good, stiff breeze?

If you want to reconstruct e-barriers to entry, where do you start?

The strongest barrier you can build is made of solid customer loyalty. This requires a commitment to hold your best customers, whatever it takes.

Netcentives developed a proprietary process to deliver airline mileage rewards for online purchasing. The currency was well understood and had clear value. Netcentives simply transferred this value to the Net and branded it for themselves and their market partners.

Developing strong customer relationships develops strong barriers to entry into your market. That can be done with reward or recognition—in fact, it's best to use both in combination and balance. You've got to make people loyal to the brand, not the bribe. You've got to make them realize how valuable they are to you, which also means making it clear to some customers that they're not valuable at all, so you've got the time and resources to shower on the most valuable customers.

The most efficient entry barrier is brandwidth. Like strong customer relationships, a strong brand creates a sturdy barrier to entry into your market. This takes more than just getting there first. It takes getting there "firstest with the mostest" and committing to holding that ground, whatever the cost.

Compared to ultrawide brandwidth and strong customer relationships, proprietary technology is a minor barrier. We apologize for the shock to the developers' self-concept. But consider the facts: First of all, while your technology might not be duplicated, it may be imitated. And will your customers really appreciate the subtler differences? In the applications software business, most products are developed with the highest-level user in mind. Yet most users access only about 20% of the program's total capability. See the world and the competitive set through your consumer's eyes.

If done well, your brand development and customer relationship development will not only position your company in the market, but also reposition all of your competitors. And you have to be ready and willing to drive differentiation with credible and relevant comparison and contrast with the competition.

This process can't stop. It's endless. You must constantly make improvements. And they must be expanding. This means always refreshing and revitalizing your brand and constantly expanding its meaning into new areas, layered on your current capabilities and consumer benefits.

This dedication to constant new news and a constant increasing of the territory of the brand is what has relentlessly built Amazon.com into a $20 billion company. Priceline.com is taking its same simple-to-understand consumer-friendly concept of "bid on perishable inventory" into another four or five or six categories.

In every category in which we've worked, we've seen the competitive array build around the early leaders: This competitive set takes the market positions "more benefit for the same price," "same benefit for the same price," "same benefit for less price," and "less benefit for a LOT less price." They splinter the market not into neat consumer segments but into the tiny fragments of individual shopping occasions.

Leaders never sit still. Leaders never allow themselves to be surrounded on the battlefield.

e-Lessons:

- Sameness kills value. So kill sameness in your product, your marketing, everything your company does.
- It all comes back to Geoffrey Moore's suggestions on cap and gap. Trying to look like and act like a leader is the way most of us have been taught to get ahead in the world. Bad advice. This is the best way to fight your way right to the middle of the pack.
- Don't act like you think a "number 1" should act. Instead be what made you a leader in the first place; act differently from your competitors, and act more meaningfully for your customers. Brands, companies, and individuals building careers all need the same building blocks of successful e-marketing: presence, relevance, clear differentiation, impeccable credibility, strong imagery.
- Increasing competition and sameness in virtually every Internet market are going to obliterate the barriers to entry into your customer franchise and your category.
- Continually broaden and deepen the meaning of your brand and the character of the relationship you establish with your customers. Nothing disassembles sameness like building brandwidth.

11

OBSOLETE YOURSELF, BEFORE SOMEBODY ELSE DOES IT FOR YOU

On the way to your site (your product, your store, your phone call), your customers are having to machete their way through an ever-growing jungle of competitive choices. They may keep coming back to you, but it's harder and harder to get there.

The sameness instinct ensures that they'll see more and more choices that look like you. **The only way to stay competitive is to constantly refresh your e-marketing. Constant innovation, making your customers expect the next new thing to be coming from you, is an important part of building brandwidth.** Successful e-marketing means constant invention and reinvention to the point of obsoleting your own market concept before the competition does it for you. It's a dog-eat-dog world out there. Don't let their dog eat yours.

Line extensions and new products are the change context of mass marketing. The upgrade is the change context of the PC world. That means the next product is not exactly new; it's just better, and it will never finish changing. The same goes for the brand. You must keep adding to it, refreshing it, building brandwidth.

Innovation on the Net is about upgrade and obsolescence. **Upgrade is an idea that is a progression on the same theme. Obsolescence is an idea that changes the theme altogether.**

In the e-market, innovating on existing market ideas is the path not just to success, but to survival. Obsoleting those old ideas (on the Net, "old" is measured in weeks and months, not years) is where the next success lies; innovation is the path to creating long-term value. Static products die.

Innovation must be a constant process in the product and in the brand and in every aspect of communicating the brand. Innovation improves on marketplace ideas, and the best of it obsoletes current market ideas. This has to be the goal in product development: an unending process of improvement with the goal of obsoleting your current idea with a better one. This is what Steve Jobs did with his development of the GUI (graphical user interface). It made personal computing easier, faster, and more accessible to more people; it was the development of point-and-click computing, obsoleting the typed-in coded commands of DOS. This repositioned Microsoft's DOS software and the IBM PC as the "harder to use" products. When you obsolete an existing marketplace idea, you instantly reposition the company behind that old idea. Microsoft was forced to step up its own development of GUI, the basis of the Windows operating system, which buried DOS forever.

Using innovation to reposition the competition is what Charles Schwab did to the idea of the full-service broker as traditionally defined by Merrill Lynch. Schwab obsoleted the idea, first with discount ("no frills") brokerage for involved investors, and then with e-trading and e-information. Though virtually all of Schwab's accounts are opened face-to-face (people like to know there is a human being at some point in the process), the Net is used as information distribution source, supplementing Schwab's BAM (bricks-and-mortar) market presence.

Merrill had assured its brokers and customers that Internet was a shaky, passing fancy. It was that familiar reactive response to the Net: "This, too, shall pass." Less than six months later, Chair David Komansky announced that Merrill would join the e-trading stampede; he announced this so abruptly that he hadn't even notified Merrill's force of full-service brokers. The result was chaos. It put Merrill in the position of having to clearly differentiate between the full-service standard and the discount and e trade within their own product and service line. That means the discount and e-trade portions of their offer essentially sell against the full-service offer, and vice versa. They have no choice: they either cannibalize their own offers or see them eaten by somebody else.

We learned in politics that the best chance for control of the dialogue in a campaign or issue debate is at the very beginning. Playing catch up, reacting to a competitor, puts them in charge of the dialogue. This thinking has put Schwab firmly in control of defining the Merrill brand. It's a scary place for Merrill to be.

Merrill is finally reacting with a strategy that may change the dialogue once more: a "Have It Your Way" strategy that allows clients to access various levels of Merrill service in any distribution mode they want. They're fighting choice and change with more choice and change. This may mark a change in the dialogue between the BAMs and the Internet services. As the BAMs become BAM.com's, they can begin to leverage their advantages of convenience, brand awareness, and existing customer franchise.

Innovation on the Net for any product changes the market for every other product. It sets a new standard that is applied beyond specific product categories and, indeed, is applied by consumers beyond the Net. Brookstone in malls and a number of companies in catalogues have built added value into their products, using compelling and engaging information. The Net makes this easier, but also makes it imperative for other marketers to make changes, particularly in the ways they use information and interaction as a value-add to their product, package, or retail experience. Many trend watchers believe that Internet commerce will overtake traditional retail, except for those retailers who concentrate on developing a branded, highly relevant, highly differentiated shopping experience.

Trial on the net is rampant; huge numbers of consumers experience innovations. And they've come to expect more and more of them. They take new expectations from those experiences wherever they go, whatever they're shopping for at the time. You don't have to be an Internet company to be affected by these changes. They're everywhere e-consumers are.

In the past century, brands became the dominant motivation of choice for all consumers in the United States. In the open marketplace at the beginning of the 1900s, choice was made strictly on the basis of the product and its seller; most products were openly displayed. Often the products were sold by their manufacturers—farmers and craftsmen. As mass manufacturing revolutionized our economy, branded products in packages (packaged goods) began to appear at the corner mom and pop store. Originally, these stores consisted of a small vestibule with a counter and a huge back room with shelves and bins filled with products. The consumer would walk to the counter and present a shopping list, mostly of items, not brands. Mom or Pop would present the list to a stock boy, who would fill the order from the backroom shelves and then present the order or deliver it to the consumer's home. This original mom and pop market design lacked something of the open display of the traditional marketplace, with its enticement to buy more than you really need. The shop owner could and would suggest additional items, but that meant guessing at the consumer's hot buttons at the moment.

The first supermarkets were micromarkets by today's standards, but they presented on open shelves a wide variety of products and often more than one brand in each category. Mass marketing made it possible to develop, distribute, and market new brands across the country—and the shelves quickly filled with competitive brands in EVERY category. SUPER supermarkets were needed to display this increasing cornucopia of choice; then superDUPER supermarkets. Interestingly, even the biggest food retailers have found that the open display of food such as fresh fruits and vegetables is still the best way to spur impulse based on motivating hunger. And even the biggest, most modern stores put fruits and vegetables at the entrance of the shopping area of the store. **In the very largest mega-food-retailers, like Sam's Clubs, the brands do the selling on their own.** They are displayed starkly on warehouse shelves, depending totally on the consumers' brand knowledge and packaging to do the motivation. In this brand-savvy, brand-saturated environment, consumers can make brand choices for themselves and order branded merchandise for home delivery.

The Internet is about change that's founded on the basics. Internet companies innovate by building on existing retailing and marketing concepts. And e-tailing borrows from almost every stage of the development of brand selling in the United States. Although the Net can't yet use display as effectively as the open market, just wait for wider and wider band transmission and 3D display. The Net uses the traditional merchant's selling style, providing information and guidance personally and even allowing bidding and haggling through auctions and reverse auctions. The Net uses customization and personalization in the way that most traditional merchants did. And yet the Internet allows infinite inventory and display.

On the Net we see a compression of traditional innovation cycles. Change that used to evolve over years now happens over months. Hundreds of millions of dollars are waged every day on the prediction of the next change. **What's driving this accelerated pace of change on the Internet and in the rest of our economy is the**

insatiable desire for choice and change among American consumers. The more choice is provided, the more it is desired.

The consumer market is made up of molecules in constant motion. Those reassuring solid bars of market share are actually teeming with those Web consumer molecules moving out of one brand franchise and into another from one usage occasion to another. Brandwidth is done one occasion at a time, so it requires constant brand marketing.

What will happen with Web portals? It's been pretty clear that bigness would dominate—aggregating the largest number of users would provide the resources to provide more services more efficiently and allow the strong to get stronger. It's been clear that there would be room at the top of that market for only two or three big players—AOL, Yahoo!, and . . . who? The big ones are developing content, promotion, advertiser relationships, and marketing partnerships based on the idea that they will control the movement of their customers on the Net.

Nevertheless BIG portal growth has slowed recently, as more sophisticated Net users move past them to more specialized, niche portals and virtual portals. Virtual portals are sites that offer a robust set of information services arrayed around their core function—for instance, e-Trade, TheStreet.com, and other financial sites. Want the latest news headlines, your local weather, e-mail, or chat? You can get those features on almost ANY site. While billions have been bet on the idea that the Web portal business will evolve like the network television business did—three huge portals with enormous control over their users—it's beginning to look a lot more like satellite TV, with infinite choices of where to enter and where to go once you do. The BIG portals are betting on the resurgence of mass marketing. **But if you've got millions to bet, bet them on choice and change.** That's the safest bet on the Net.

The real value on the Net now is content, engaging consumers with superior information and entertainment, creating user relationships that are lasting and valuable. To succeed in getting a greater share of the consumer's time, which means value, you have to be able to overcome this powerful force of the desire for choice and change. Your idea has to be so compelling, personal, and customized to the e-consumer's needs that you overcome the basic value concept of the Net, which is choice and change. All Net consumers are on virtual Rollerblades; catching them is not easy. The stronger your pull of personalization, the smaller your audience is likely to be. And even once you find the content that holds an audience, no matter how small, you must be ready to constantly refresh and innovate in order to hold their attention. One thing you can never rely on is that your customers won't be aware of other choices in the marketplace. You've got to win in a constant, free-for-all competition.

The only way you innovate on choice is with more personal choice. The BIG portals will win only by expanding choice, not by narrowing it. We live in a world of confident consumers. They feel quite capable of making choices for themselves. The power of letting them develop their own choices is quite obvious on the Net. More and more services allow Web consumers to develop a customized service for themselves: five times more users return to MyExcite than to Excite.

The major television networks were built on a model of limited choice, but change overwhelmed them, and they were enveloped into big media companies that have gotten bigger by expanding choice. They can never stop.

Disney, for example, has tried again and again to formularize its success. It doesn't work. There's no more money to be made in distributing the same old stuff farther and farther—it's already reached every corner of the globe. The overdistribution of undervalued stuff has hurt the Disney brand already (the same old script with new characters in their now annual animated films and the same old toys and games licensed in their wake). Disney adopted the Lucas

Film model of using the release of the film as a catalyst for the release of action figures and other toys related to the film, and the revenues from these related products far exceeded those from the film itself. This essentially established the model for the rest of the entertainment industry and the toy industry. It was a model most industry planners assumed would go on indefinitely. Toy retailers and the marketers who promoted with Disney certainly hoped so, too.

But the model had diminishing returns over time. First, everybody followed Disney into the practice. Every week there were new toys from movies and TV shows kids had barely heard about. Certainly they hadn't learned the story lines and couldn't figure out how to play with many of the toys—who was the good guy and who was the bad guy? Industry quality control was slipping week to week. And Disney had their own quality problems. The push to keep the movies coming seemed to dilute their quality and specialness. Because of the need to create the toy factory out of the movie, the creative content was limited to traditional heroes and villains, limiting the innovation of the Disney Imagineers. The coup de grace for this model may have been the sweeping deal between Disney and McDonald's, which put a Disney toy in every Happy Meal bag. These are high-quality action figures—it's hard to imagine kids going to Toys R Us to spend their hard-earned allowance on a $9 action figure that they can get free at McDonald's. Though the model may be broken, it certainly hasn't been improved on. The industry just keeps trying to stamp out the same model, movie after movie. And it's just not working.

Renewal for the Disney brand won't be achieved by increased distribution or optimization of current creative assets: It's about creating new creative assets by real innovation, obsoleting the old ones, not just trotting them out for another round of promotion.

The irony is that Disney does this so well in their theme parks, constantly developing new ideas and refreshing old ones. This constant change (along with their operational excellence) is why they've been able to hold customers for repeat visits. Neither the consumer products division nor the entertainment division seems to be working off that same innovation-focused strategy. They could learn a lot from a visit to Disney World. Net technology can show Disney the way out of its current mess. It can allow them to understand their customers better. It will allow them to connect smaller interest groups of their customers and serve them more personally, creating deeper value in narrower spaces. It's the end of mass market Disney. But it could be the beginning of "My Disney" for a new generation of parents and kids. They can still market broadly, but must appeal narrowly. And they have to keep changing and changing and changing.

Innovation doesn't just mean opening a new movie based on the old format. Innovate means NEW. When we worked with Fox, the insurgent television network that innovated with shows like *In Living Color, The Simpsons,* and *The X-Files,* we put up a sign in president David Hill's office: "When we take a chance, we win." Hill is now back in control of Fox Sports, where he's been a brilliant innovator. Indeed, when he began putting the Fox Sports logo on screen with the game score and other information, the change was so controversial that the Los Angeles Police Department granted him the right to a bodyguard. Now that look is everywhere in televised sports. Sports consumers' reaction has been, "Next change, please."

Winning formulas don't keep winning in this new environment, either on or off the Net. Leadership is more perishable than ever (again, we're talking about weeks, not years). Levi's recent struggles have shown the change in what used to be a key big brand dynamic—authenticity. When consumers are confident, they value newness over tradition, innovation over authenticity.

So you have to move fast in order to get ahead of your competition, and then you quickly have to change to win again and again. The old adage was "eat lunch or be lunch," and to some degree it's still true. But the advice today is more like "eat lunch and then be your *own* lunch."

The most important innovations are for your own customers, not to attract new ones. It's a necessity to constantly keep your relationship with your customers fresh and alive. You must refresh your site; your products, services, and support; and your relationship builders at a pace that recognizes the wants and needs of your best customers, not just the occasional browsers. FedEx was growing ahead of UPS because they allowed the older company to become the insurgent in innovation. Now FedEx is acting like the incumbent, failing to move quickly to the Internet opportunity (somebody's got to deliver all that stuff). UPS was on top of these changes and is pulling out ahead in its plain brown wrapper trucks.

In the e-marketing era, you must constantly question the relevance, the validity, the specialness of your product or service—or someone else will, often ripping off the very model, design, or innovation that you were still patting yourself on the back for and then improving on it before you do.

The Internet has sped up the pace of change for you and your company, whether you're online or not. And that's one reason why the acceptable level of growth in any category is almost always underestimated by the incumbents. These incumbents are quite satisfied with the usual slow, steady growth in their market (after all, slow, steady market growth always benefits the incumbent most).

The level of acceptable growth has been changed by Net insurgents and their innovations. They estimate vast potential in new markets, where the incumbents just don't see it, just don't get it. A brisk environment of innovative change creates vitality that wasn't there before.

Maxwell House, Folgers, and their parents had contented themselves with a no-growth coffee market in the United States. The penetration of coffee drinking in the U.S. population in 1960 was 70%, with virtually every man, woman, and dog in America drinking 3.2

cups of java per day. By 1988, penetration was down to 50% and consumption was 1.7 cups per day. At that point, the major companies adopted strategies to "manage the decline" of the industry. Needless to say, that strategic attitude doesn't create a vital and creative culture. In the "managing down" mode, these companies put all their energies into developing bribes (okay, promotions) to get people to decline in consumption a little more slowly.

Starbucks saw the market differently. They saw opportunity in the market through product change, specialization, and customization, by extending the brand image of the product to the environment in which it is consumed. They saw mountains of opportunity (and proved they were not a mirage), where the big coffee marketers saw only a desert of decline. Their optimism was fulfilled by their redefinition of the business and reengagement of consumers. The results have been remarkable, not just for Starbucks, but for the entire industry, Folgers, Maxwell House, Juan Valdez, and the donkey he rode in on. Penetration is now upward of 76%, and per capita consumption is up to 3.6 cups per day. All this, without significantly increasing consumption in the home. They innovated the idea of coffee and coffee drinking to the extent of obliterating the old model.

Microsoft pioneered this kind of model in software. The company focused its marketing on its installed base. Its marketing was established in "depth and breadth," selling the same people more improvements on the same product ("The product is never finished") and selling those same customers more products along the Microsoft line ("No sale is ever final"). This made constant dialogue and a developing relationship with Microsoft customers necessary.

eBay has done the most outstanding job of using innovation to activate an inert but latent market: selling old stuff. The stuff of garage and church rummage sales has sat in attics and overstuffed, dusty garages for years. eBay redefines it in value. SOMEBODY out there is looking for that fondue pot. And you could get that Mickey

Mouse waffle iron you've always wanted. The Internet allows eBay to find those disparate e-consumers: The garage sale drives to you!

Every marketer wants early adopters, the highly influential users of everything from beer to sneakers to cars to mouthwash to stocks and bonds to military weaponry. The key is to realize that they, too, are self-selecting. They are constantly looking for new ideas, brands, and products to try. **So the good news about constant innovation and obsolescence is that although it may seem exhausting and expensive, every time you upgrade or obsolete your own product or service, you are creating a new opportunity to win customers away from the competitor that isn't doing it.** Your customers soon anticipate that the best changes will come from you. And that's the way you build brandwidth with them.

The true innovator, the one who obsoletes the current market model, is like the political insurgent who redefines the dialogue in a political campaign. That's what John McCain did in his short but impactful run for the Republican nomination in 2000. Controlling the dialogue is the key objective of any political campaign. The candidate who controls the dialogue controls the context of the campaign, defines "what this election is all about," that is, the issues debated and the pace of change of those issues. That candidate, invariably, wins.

This is the model of innovation and obsolescence you want to follow. This is the objective you want to achieve in your market, whatever it is you do, make, and sell: Control the dialogue.

Arc, or Allied Riser Corporation, provides the "last mile" connection of fiber optic cable into office buildings. Their marketplace is a huge playing field holding all the options for Internet connection, from dial-up to optics. Most consumers are unclear about the differences between and the benefits of the many options. Arc has worked effectively to narrow the dialogue to one issue: speed. It's an e-consumer benefit that is easily demonstrable and highly relevant to heavy business users, and it happens to play to their strength.

There's a final point about innovation. Some companies who are very good at many other things are just not good at innovation. And they're not likely to get good at it any time soon. The problem may be organizational or cultural. Many huge market leaders just have trouble thinking like two kids in a garage somewhere with nothing to lose.

Those kids in the garage don't look, act, think, or even smell like you do. They can't manage a multitiered organization, or complex manufacturing processes, or a global distribution network. But they can kick innovating ass. They innovate because they don't know any better. How do you compete with them?

What to do if you're a Starbucks? You broke the mold in your industry; you were Mr. and Mrs. New Ideas. You were the coffee business skunk works. At least, that's what you were about a thousand stores ago. Now you're too busy stamping out a success model to invent a new one. Meantime, schools of baby sharks—Starbucks knockoffs, mom and pop delis that now sell latte and frappucino, the more exotic McDonald's drive-thru—are circling, working up the strength and courage for an all-out attack on you. Fighting them off, where do you find the time to look for innovation, and how do you get the space to think about obsoleting yourself?

What do you do if you're stuck in a big, staid BAM with no history of innovation, no skunk works, and no kids in garages?

1 **Stop thinking about the competition as competition. Think about the competition, particularly these smaller, do-or-die competitors, as your friends. Think of them as R&D.** They're likely to be thinking up your next great idea. The reinvention of Starbucks probably won't be invented at headquarters in Seattle. More likely, it will be invented someplace else in this caffeine-starved country—by one of those baby shark competitors. The question is, will the baby sharks—the kids in the garage—know how really great their innovation is? And will

they know how to capitalize on it? The most successful innovators among big marketing organizations have been unabashed thieves of fledgling concepts.

2 **Don't look for innovation just in your company.** Find it anywhere you can find it. Look into other categories for inspiration. If you're in sporting goods, look in fashion or automotive; if you're in soda pop, look in software. Expect to find it among smaller, hungrier competitors in any category.

3 **Don't be proud. Innovation is not invention.** It's making a new invention actually work. Just remember this: Coke didn't invent cola; Microsoft didn't invent the operating system; McDonald's didn't invent fast food. "First mover," that key Internet designation, is not just about arriving at an idea first, but about taking control of it first and getting it right. That's market innovation.

e-Lessons:

☐ In today's e-market innovation isn't an event—it's a way of doing business. And it's like heroin. Once you start, you can't stop. But THIS heroin happens to be good for you.

☐ Focus innovation on your own customers first, to build brandwidth and give them more reasons to come back more often to buy more. Constantly refresh your offer to them.

☐ The point of innovation is obsolescence—the goal is to obsolete your old market idea with a totally new one by the process of constant innovation. If you don't obsolete yourself, the competition will be happy to do it for you.

☐ Look for innovative ideas anywhere you can find them. Don't be self-conscious about borrowing somebody else's concept and improving on it.

□ For Web and non-Web companies an attempt at relevant differentiation means tacking on additional product or service features, but these often conflict with the original DNA of the product, its basic concept. They end up diluting its brand meaning. Look at all the drugstore sites. What's the USP (unique selling proposition) of each of them? What's the difference between PlanetRX.com, drkoop.com, CVS.com, and all the rest? Don't strain yourself; there isn't any. In adding features you have to be extremely careful that you don't obliterate the original and more unique idea in search of being competitive with more "robust" services. Stick to your knitting.

12

DESTINATION IS THE WHOLE ENCHILADA

We've got a lot of problems with the airline industry. You may have guessed that by now. Familiarity breeds contempt. And we have a whole lot of contempt based on our multimillion miles on commercial airliners. To put it simply: They have forgotten their customers. In fact, most of the time, they forget they even HAVE customers. Yes, there are some shining moments on Southwest and Continental and British Airways, but, by and large, these airline people don't even recognize they're in the customer business. The job of an airline employee is to fly a plane, repair an engine, work the computer at the podium, serve meals and drinks, load bags, or sell tickets. And it would all be sooo much easier if it weren't for the damned passengers. We've found airline management to be virtually advice-proof on the subject of customer relations. They take suggestions like Sonny Liston used to take punches.

But there's one thing the airlines do that DOESN'T upset us. You walk up to the ticket counter and they immediately ask, "Where are you going?"

Seems like a perfectly reasonable question. You can't go anywhere without a destination in mind, right? But why is it when we ask that question of our clients, especially those on the Web, they look at us like they just swallowed a couple of anchovies? "Huh? What do you mean?"

"We mean, where are you going?"

They don't have the faintest idea where they're going. Yes, they know they want to disintermediate some process or create some new vertical marketplace or develop some software enabling the e-supply chain. But they don't really know where they're going, and they don't even want to talk about it. That's why so many of them get lost so quickly. While wandering around from task to task and program to program, they lose their way. They lose the meaning of their brand, lose the heart of their customer franchise, or get eaten by a competitor who DOES know where they're going and what it will take to get there. It's not just that they hit a bump in the road and lose control of the steering wheel. It's not that they fail and then don't know what to do. Failure makes it very easy to know what to do. It narrows your options to subleasing the office and posting your resume on ComputerJobs.com. "Nothing clarifies the mind like knowing you're going to be shot in the morning," Churchill said.

Many Web companies get lost while succeeding. Without a clear sense of destination, they get just as disoriented by success as by failure. You've seen it again and again—a Web company achieves a shining moment of success, but the shining seems to freeze them like headlights do a deer on the highway. And opportunity swerves right around them. They get left behind.

The good companies, on the Web or off it, know where they're going. They have a clear sense of destination. And they stay focused on it until they get to the promised land.

This isn't about writing a corporate vision statement. We've seen several thousand of them in our careers, most of them pretty bad and almost all of them interchangeable. You can nail a generic one up on almost anybody's wall. And if you take the words "excellence" and "superior" and "customer" out of them, they'd fall over. Vision statements are great things for the inside cover of the annual report, but they're not great things to guide a company into the future. For that you need a defined destination. **You need to know exactly where you're going to know how you're going to get there.** Everybody in the company and everybody who supports the company must know that destination. They've got to be able to see it. Ronald Reagan called it "that shining city on the hill." They've got to want to get there.

Defining your company and brand destination is the first and maybe most important step in corporate planning and marketing strategy development. And please don't tell us you just want be the market leader. Who doesn't want to be the market leader? The question is, what will the world look like when you are the market leader? And the next question is, how are you going to get to that new world? **Destination isn't a wish—it's a definition of the way the world will be in three to five years and where you'll fit into it.** Coming up with this definition is not a creative exercise; it's a strategic process.

DEFINE YOUR DESTINY

The first issue is to define the future three to five years out. This also can't be done by wishful thinking: "I see a market for croquet wickets that's constantly expanding and we're right at the top of it!"

Defining the future is serious business and must be done with serious purpose and objectivity, using the best available information from market research, trend research, and analysts' projections. Since nobody has 20/20 foresight, it's a good idea to define more than one possible future. This is sometimes called "scenario planning." Who's doing this well? A great example comes from one of the brickest of the BAM (bricks and mortar) industries, the newspaper business:

John Oppedahl, publisher and CEO of the *Arizona Republic,* led his company in an extensive scenario planning process to define the future and their destination in it. "The mark of a great company is one that questions its future long before that future becomes questionable," he said.

Oppedahl is an unusual character in his business (and would be in any business). Many newspaper managers would rather not think about a future that might see the industry continue to lose relevance among its readers and advertisers, so they plan in a state of denial and simply project the status quo. They're certainly not unique in this. Lots of corporate managers are guilty of denial—and they're as guilty of it on the Net (where they would much rather not have to think about the "r" word . . . "revenues") as in the BAM world. The problem is that this blinds them to the real and present dangers their organizations face and, even worse, to the opportunities out there to reverse that inexorable slide of relevance.

With the help of a consulting group called Global Business Networks, John and his large team of strategists (he thinks strategy is too important to be left just to corporate strategists, just as we think marketing is too important to be left just to the marketing people) developed three possible futures for the *Arizona Republic* and the world in which it operates. The scenarios were defined in great detail, focusing not just on the newspaper and its direct competitors, but on their customers and advertisers. What world would they be living in? How would their lives be changing in the future, and where could the *Arizona Republic's* information brands fit into their needs and wants? The three scenarios were titled Steady Time (a world in which there is a lag between a customer's need and a market solution), Real Time (a world in which the market creates solutions at the same time customers have a need), and Zero Time (a world in which the market creates solutions before the customer has expressed a need). They accepted a number of givens about the future of their community, but they also took into account two critical uncertainties about their own future:

1 How fast will the Internet change business models for media and retail?
2 How long will there be a sufficient demand for mass media products from both our advertisers and readers?

There was objectivity in the team's work and a willingness to confront the most difficult future scenario. In developing these scenarios, Oppedahl's group learned a lot about where they were now as a business and community institution and a lot about how they'd have to change to become more, not less, relevant in each of the possible futures. They created a list of imperatives to win in the new economy:

◻ Act fast.
◻ Live in all three scenarios.
◻ Invest in the long term.
◻ Continue to provide excellent journalism.
◻ Commit to print for as long as it makes sense.
◻ Grow our online business.
◻ Reward innovation and risk taking.
◻ Figure out what we should stop doing.

Looking closely at these possible futures allowed them to develop business objectives that were quite a departure from the past (and from most other newspapers).

The folks at the *Arizona Republic* don't believe they can predict the future. But they do believe they can prepare for its possibilities a lot better than they have in the past and a lot better than their online or offline competition will. Newspapers are supposed to be hidebound in their management and approach to planning, but this one certainly hasn't been. And it shows in their results now and will show even more dramatically in the future. **You may work in a spanking new dot.com, but is your company doing this much to define its own future?**

You must inform your definition of the future with the best information you can lay your hands on. Add to that research and trend information your own best estimates of possible changes within your own industry. Develop more than one possible future. Who'd have predicted with certainty the development of business-to-business e-commerce in the past three years? Who'd have predicted that AOL would be taking over Time-Warner? Draw this picture of tomorrow in the greatest detail you can, so that you can see and feel it.

DEFINE YOUR PLACE IN THE FUTURE

Your company or brand destination will be determined by your definition of the position it will have in the lives of your customers in the possible future scenarios you've developed. Given your understanding of the future and based on your current and projected capabilities, this positioning will be defined partly by force and partly by aspiration: "What MUST we be?" "What do we WANT to be?" But this definition—and this is exactly what destination is all about—is not about possible outcomes; it's about the certainty of where you will be.

As we've mentioned more than once in this book, Steve Case has defined AOL's presence in the future as ubiquitous as the telephone but infinitely more useful. This makes it very clear what role AOL will have (MUST have) in the lives of its users. Robert Woodruff was the architect of the Coca-Cola worldwide bottling system for five decades. His destination for that global network was simple: "A Coke within an arm's length of desire." Every consumer on earth could get a Coke as soon as he or she wanted one. That provided a crystal-clear place for his system in the future of its customers' lives. And Bill Gates's destination for Microsoft is to help build its category into relevance for all people: "A computer on every desk, in every home." The jihad for Microsoft is both to grow with an industry and to speed the growth and deepen its effect.

These destinations are clear. Anyone at or connected to AOL, Coke, or Microsoft could understand them and understand his or her own role in helping the company get to that destination. As an aggressive packaged-goods marketer we once worked with used to say: "It's helpful to wake up in the morning knowing who you have to kill today."

So ask yourself and your team these questions about your company:

☐ Where are you going?
☐ What must you be in order to succeed—and what must you be in order to survive?
☐ Where will you fit in the lives of your customers?
☐ Where will you fit in the market of that future, among all competitors?
☐ How will you be relevant to the customers and differentiated from the competitive set?

Destination is everything. Today, you can't waste the energy of even one step in the wrong direction. You want a definition that is clear to all of your employees, shareholders, and other "friends and family." Can they see it? Is this destination a compelling promised land to them? It has to be a big black **X** on the map of tomorrow; this is where the treasure is buried.

It's not just the whole corporation that gets lost. Inside any company there are a number of activities that wander in the wilderness year after year.

"Why are you doing that?"

"We do it because that's what we do. We do it because that's the way we've always done it."

Admit it, you've seen this in your own company. We've certainly seen it in most companies—a good portion of their programmatic activities in any given year are bumping around without direction. How many activities are conducted as if you were driving down the interstate with your eyes fixed on the rearview mirror instead of the road ahead? That's what happens when you base this year's marketing plan on last year's plan or even last year's results. **The key question in planning is not what we've done, but what we WILL BE doing.** How do we get to our destination? Will you keep your eyes on the prize and the road ahead that will get you to it?

How many activities are conducted in your company with your focus fixed on the rear bumper of your chief competitor just ahead? Many a company has followed their market leader right off a cliff by doing that.

Define the future. Then define your place in it. Now you have a destination. Now you know where you're going. But how are you going to get there?

DRAW THE ROAD MAP

Once you know the destination—and ONLY once you know the destination—you can begin to draw the road map to get there. This is really what strategic planning is all about.

We used to get frustrated trying to explain the strategic planning process to client groups. Finally, we'd ask, "Who knows what they're going to do when they retire?"

In a group of about a dozen people, maybe one would raise his or her hand. One time it was a guy who said he and his wife wanted to become pig farmers. Once the chuckles subsided, we asked, "So what are you doing to make it happen?"

"Well, we've bought land in southern Ohio . . . a hundred-acre farm. We've studied the pig farming business—my wife has done courses in animal husbandry and farm management at the local ag college. We've worked on a business plan . . . outbuildings, feed, pigs and stuff. And we know the magic number we need to make it happen."

"Bingo! That's strategic planning."

The destination was clearly defined in the minds of this wife and husband. They had a point to reach and were precise about the roads they would travel to get there. The fact is, it's pretty hard to develop strategy without destination. Yes, strategies will follow a set of objectives. But where do the objectives lead you? You need a final destination that will define why everybody does what he or she does within your organization.

Defining destination ensures that your strategic development will be focused forward, not backward. It ensures that your strategic development will be focused on the world of your customers and not your competitors. This process of defining destination keeps you honest.

We've emphasized again and again the importance of controlling the dialogue in your market. The player who controls the market dialogue invariably wins the market leadership. It gives you the jump on every competitor. If you're the player with the best-formed view of the future, you're likely to be able to shape the direction of your market. If you know where you're going, you're going to be moving in the market with the least wind resistance, with the most efficiency and effectiveness. Destination is the whole enchilada.

BROADCAST YOUR DESTINATION

Once you've defined your company and brand destination, you must communicate it loud and clear. You must communicate it inside out. You must communicate it all the time, in everything you do and say.

- ☐ Start by defining the destination to your own employees. Make sure they understand and embrace the definition. This IS that shining city on the hill. This IS the promised land. They must not only understand and embrace this concept, but be committed to communicating it outward. They've got to become missionaries.
- ☐ Communicate destination to your shareholders and market partners, the "friends and family" of your company and brand. Defining destination is like defining brand: Make sure the definition is relevant and differentiated; make sure it has rational and emotional benefits; draw it with rich imagery. Make it so real they can touch it.
- ☐ Communicate your destination to your customers. In doing so, you are helping define their own world (and, in the process, defining your inseparable place in it). Give the destination finite shape: If there's a product destination inherent in this definition, consider developing design models. (Think of the effect of "concept cars" developed by the big auto makers: "There's a Ford in your future.")
- ☐ Communicate your destination within your market. This shows your commitment to succeed, and it creates a sense of

manifest destiny. If your definition of the future is objective and well informed, it will influence your competitors as well as your friends. Yes, it gives them the opportunity to try to position themselves in the way of your destination, but it often has the effect of forcing them to believe they must follow you into tomorrow. "The battle must be won before it is fought," said the Chinese military strategist Sun Tzu. That's how you do it. Allow the uncommitted in your marketplace—the analysts and journalists—to jump on the bandwagon. As we've said many times to our clients, **the most powerful emotion on the Internet is inevitability.** If your destination provides a compelling concept, it can be used to win over key objective audiences in the market.

Destination is not just the whole enchilada, but the whole Combo Plate with salsa and sour cream. It's all here. Define your brand destination. Do it successfully and you will win. Define the future well and you will own it.

e-Lessons:

☐ Destination is the foundation for all planning. You've got to develop strategy with a clear sense of where you're going.

☐ Start by defining the future—and probably more than one possible future. What will the world be like for your customers? What will the market be like for you and your customers? Be objective and use the best available information to define future scenarios.

☐ Define your brand's position in the future. That's destination. How will you uniquely fit into your customers' needs and desires? What must you and will you do to achieve success with them?

☐ Develop the strategic road map toward your defined destination. Base the plan on the future, not on the past. Focus it on your customers, not on your competitors.

☐ Communicate your destination aggressively with ALL audiences, inside and outside the company. Make it a goal to have your definition of the future accepted in your market. Lobby for your future. And never stop working toward it in everything you do.

EPILOGUE: THE BEGINNING OF MARKETING AS WE WILL KNOW IT

This book is meant to be YOUR personal road map toward a destination of success on your terms.

Along the way, we hope we've convinced you to create your exciting new marketing plans on the strong old pillars of business fundamentals. e-Marketing is marketing. And all marketing is serious business. What's true on the Net will be true on Main Street. e-Consumers are changing the way business and marketing will be done on and off the Net. And as the BAMs (bricks and mortars) develop and implement their own Internet strategies and integrate them into their total business strategies comprehensively (so far, they're mostly still kept off to the side, like an outhouse), there will be yet another major transition with the development of the BAM.coms.

Like we've said again and again and again, if you're going to be right, the smart money will be on continuing change in all markets and on the continuing attraction of choice for all consumers.

Get the basics down, and only THEN get creative. Picasso was a master draftsman. Miles Davis was an accomplished tactical musician.

You can't improvise on improvisation—you improvise on the basics.

Keep your eye on the road ahead. Never look back. Never let the competition take your focus off your own customers and the destination you define as your place in their lives. You can't let up. The lazy days of marketing are long gone. More and more companies and investors will be turning to marketing to make the difference, to get the results they need as more changes and more choices come online. They'll be turning to you. And we want you to be ready.

INDEX

Over the past 30+ years, Sergio Zyman has honed, tested, and continually improved upon his strong beliefs about what marketing is and how it should be used to build brands and drive businesses. This work included serving as Chief Marketing Officer of the Coca-Cola Company, where worldwide annual volume grew from 9 to 15 billion cases behind his leadership, the most explosive growth period in the company's history. Sergio is currently founder and CEO of Z Marketing, a multifaceted marketing strategy firm focused on empowering world-class marketing. Sergio can be contacted by e-mail at *sergio@zmarketing.com*.

For more information and assistance on how you can achieve world-class marketing results in your business, visit ZMarketing. com.